UNjust

Gary Ivory

Copyright © 2021 Gary Ivory
All rights reserved
First Edition

NEWMAN SPRINGS PUBLISHING
320 Broad Street
Red Bank, NJ 07701

First originally published by Newman Springs Publishing 2021

ISBN 978-1-63881-357-6 (Paperback)
ISBN 978-1-63881-358-3 (Hardcover)
ISBN 978-1-63881-359-0 (Digital)

Printed in the United States of America

Contents

Introduction 5
Acknowledgments 9

Off to the Races 11
Muh's Baby Boy 21
Homecoming 31
Calm Before the Storm.. 37
Free at Last... 51
Never Give Up!.. 67
Things Fall Apart 76
Determination 82
Easter.. 88
The Darkest Hour.. 93
Georgia on My Mind 103
On the Battlefield 108
New Year 114
Glimmer of Hope... 119
On the Run 127
Turning Around 134
Do No Harm.. 139
Keep the Faith.. 144
Amber Alert 154
Redemption 160
Verdict 164
Justice 189

No Way Out 197
A Final Word 204

Resources 211
Websites 213

> "But as for you, you meant evil against me;
> but God meant it for good."
> —Genesis 50:20 NKJV

Introduction

I did not intend to write this book. I only wrote it after wrestling with a painful series of events beginning in 1999.

I had spent most of my professional life working with a nonprofit organization dedicated to reforming the juvenile and criminal justice, child welfare and other public systems. I had traveled the country developing effective alternatives to incarceration for young people. I did not expect to become a victim of crimes perpetrated against me by my ex-girlfriend.

Beginning in 1999, I experienced firsthand how "biased" the criminal justice and other public systems are in far too many cases. I was a victim of horrific crimes, yet I was treated as a perpetrator.

It all began in 1999 near Dallas, Texas. I met Lisa Brown (Lauryn Burns in the book), who would become my daughter's mother. It began innocently, but quickly degenerated into an intense relationship that was difficult to bear. I lived in constant fear that she would kill or do great harm to my family and me. It was her way or the highway. The ability to negotiate was nonexistent. It was sixteen years of living in absolute fear. Sixteen years of victimization. Sixteen years of relentless trauma. Sixteen years of fighting for my daughter across many states. Sixteen years of threats made against me and many others. Sixteen years of massive system failure. Sixteen years of a living hell!

We met when I lived in Baltimore, Maryland, and she lived in Dallas, Texas. I knew that there was something wrong with her when I met her, but I didn't know at the time that Lisa had a long history of severe mental illness. I would later come to find that she suffered from borderline personality disorder, narcissistic personality disorder, and schizoaffective disorder.

Lisa had a difficult childhood that began in the housing developments of Chicago and Houston. She overcame many of these childhood adversities, earned a master's degree, and was a successful engineer and math teacher. Everything looked great on the outside, but inside was a raging volcano waiting to erupt! Her mental illness negatively impacted the lives of hundreds, or even thousands of people whom she victimized and tormented.

Throughout those sixteen years, Lisa threatened and manipulated judges, prosecutors, defense attorneys, social workers, lawyers, detectives, police, psychologists, psychiatrists, colleagues, school administrators, and the guardian ad litem assigned to our case. She used her vehicle as a lethal weapon. She was seductive and smart. She was cunning and confident. She was resilient and recalcitrant. She was filled with ambiguities and complexities that caused others to fear and loathe her.

She convinced many people that she was a compassionate and caring mother of our daughter while she privately abused her and tormented me and my family. She charmed NFL football players into dating her and supporting her extravagant lifestyle. She also dated her attorney who would have done anything to keep her out of prison. Her attorney was both her lover and her lawyer!

My family and I constantly lived in fear that she would kill us or have us killed. She was violent but made it appear that we were the violent ones. She could manufacture tears as well as any Hollywood actress.

The story begins in Dallas but leads to legal battles across many states. Amber alerts are issued as Lisa kidnaps Sommer (Sophia in the book), changes her name, dresses her in a hijab, and drives from Texas through Oklahoma, Missouri, Indiana, and Illinois.

The FBI becomes involved as Lisa's mental health deteriorates. This book reveals the extreme measures to which a father will go to save his daughter and sheds light on public systems that let them both down repeatedly.

This is a story that is far too familiar and common. A father seeking to have a relationship with his daughter gets treated unjustly and unfairly. A criminal justice system doesn't apply the principle of equal justice under the law. A legal system fails to adhere to the grand principle of presumption of innocence. A family court system that often doesn't act in the best interest of the child. A Child Protective Services system fails to protect a vulnerable child. A corrupt attorney allows his lover and client to run afoul of the law. A prosecutor pursues convictions over justice and fairness. A judge releases a woman from jail who is both homicidal and suicidal. A scorned woman destroys countless lives with reckless abandon. A high-conflict custody battle goes terribly wrong!

She was on the run with our daughter for many years. I was considered the "monster" while she lived a luxurious lifestyle in Dallas, Houston, Atlanta and Chicago. While I petitioned the courts, she used her looks and lies to manipulate the system. It worked for many years until things began to turn around. This is the story of how the persistence of a father paid off and a once-traumatized child overcame adversity.

Acknowledgments

I want to thank so many people without whom this book would not have been possible. First, to my deceased mother and father, Charlie Mae Searcy Ivory and Wesley Ivory: Thanks for bringing me into this world and teaching me grit and determination. To my wife, Christie: Thanks for being the love of my life. Thanks for your persistence and tireless support. Thanks to my daughter, Sommer, who has endured so much pain and trauma. Yet, you are resilient and an overcomer! Thanks to my daughters, Madison, and Mallory: Thanks for staying strong and resilient! You have overcome much. Thanks to my sister, Brenda, for encouraging me to tell the story many years ago.

In loving memory of my deceased siblings and close relatives: C.E. Maureen, Mary, Wanda, Theodore "Sonny," Anthony "Preacher," and Shirley. I will see each of you on the other side.

Many thanks to the tireless support of the late Tom Jeffers. Also, many thanks to Minette Bauer and Jeff Fleischer for their tireless support.

This is a work of nonfiction. Certain names have been changed, and some dialogue has been edited.

Off to the Races

The Texas heat was resplendent and balmy in the spring of 1999. The intense heat belied the incessant joy of being home. I had relocated from Texas to reside in Baltimore in early 1997. I had moved to Baltimore to begin yet another leadership journey. I had completed a fellowship and was working at a national foundation that developed low-income housing.

I had always preferred living on the East Coast as we often referred to it. I had longed to get back home to Texas to visit with my ailing mother. All of us called my mother "Muh," short for Madea. Muh still lived in the small East Texas town of Pittsburg where I had grown up. During my trips back home, I would often visit with Muh, then stop to visit friends who lived in nearby Fort Worth.

On this trip back home, I decided to hang out with my good friends: Mark, Antoine and Reggie. We had been close friends since the early 1990s. We had stayed in contact after I had moved from Fort Worth to Baltimore.

My trip back home had been uneventful. On a hot and humid Friday night, my friends and I decided to attend a "Kappa" party at Lone Star Park, a horseracing track near Dallas and a gathering place for social events. I looked forward to going with my friends to the fraternity party.

We met up at Mark's apartment and rode together. Although we weren't related, many people thought we were brothers. Mark, Antoine, Reggie, and I were "thicker than thieves" as we used to say. We were all Black men who had overcome much adversity. We were in our late 20's at the time.

Once we arrived at the party, I bought a round of drinks for the fellas. A few libations and we were ready to celebrate.

While standing at the bar chatting, a woman on the dance floor caught my attention. She was dressed provocatively and dancing alone. She danced suggestively as she swayed to the music. She had on a black skirt with high heels and a suggestive red top. She stood out so much that people on and off the dance floor stared at her. She was in her own world. I continued to watch her with great interest. I always liked women who were a bit "non-traditional."

After a while, I turned to my friends and asked, "What do you think, fellas?" referring to the woman I had been watching on the dance floor.

"Man, leave that woman alone…there is something wrong with her," intoned Mark, Antoine, and Reggie in unison.

Those words of caution didn't stop me from approaching her. Instead, they piqued my interest even more. As the party wound down for the night, I saw her once again on the dance floor. I walked up to her and introduced myself.

"My name is Gerald, and yours?"

"My name is Lauryn," she said in a soft and sensuous voice.

"I have been watching you dance for a while on the dance floor. Can I buy you a drink?" I asked.

"No, I don't drink, but where are you from?" she asked.

"I live in Baltimore, but I grew up in East Texas. I am in town to see my mother. She is sick, and I am in town to visit with her. I am just hanging out in Dallas with friends before going back to Baltimore. Where are you from?" I asked inquisitively.

"Chicago. Well, I am from Chicago by way of Houston. I am living in Dallas now. I am an engineer at Texas Technology here in Dallas."

Texas Technology was a leading technology firm that specialized in developing calculators and other emerging technologies.

I was smitten. She seemed smart. She could hold up her end of a great conversation. She had flowing, almond-colored hair that lay softly down her caramel-colored back. She had piercing brown eyes that softly coaxed and seduced me into a trance. Her clothing suited her well-proportioned, curvaceous body.

She was also well-educated and erudite. She made it known that she was a world traveler and spoke several languages. She had been active in theater. That seemed like a winning combination. We continued to talk until the party ended. I walked Lauryn to her car. We gave one another an embrace, and I left to meet up with my friends.

Once I got into the car, my friends were beside themselves.

"Gerald, you know she is crazy, right?" Reggie was always the first to speak up.

I didn't want to hear their negative criticism. She seemed a bit weird, but nothing to be that concerned about, at least so I thought.

They kept mentioning how different she seemed to them.

"Man, I would be careful if I were you. Something is not right with her," Antoine said with great angst.

Those words of caution rang hollow that night. She seemed to have a lot going for her. She fit the bill.

Meeting Lauryn that Friday night would haunt me for many years to come. What was it about her that was so interesting? What made me keep pursuing and entertaining her even after my friends' warnings and my own internal reservations? Maybe I liked her because she was just different. Whatever the reason, I would soon come to find that meeting her would have lifelong consequences.

The next morning, I drove back to East Texas to visit Muh again before my trip back to Baltimore.

I loved the scenic drive to East Texas. The lush green vegetation and tall pine trees belied the harsh realities facing my family. Despite the pain of its history, East Texas held a sublime beauty. Pittsburg had many redeeming qualities. My childhood was chock-full of fond memories. We found beauty in play, in adventure, in church, and in the many people who loved us. Unconditional love saved us. It is the only thing that ever does.

Despite the challenges in my childhood, Pittsburg was home. I had an enduring love for my family and the many people who helped me surmount difficult obstacles. I would often say many years later that I had broken the rearview mirror when I left my hometown. I was looking forward to the opportunities that lay before me. I didn't want to look backward, but forward.

I always found great joy whenever I saw Muh. My sister, Maria, had called and told me a few months before that the doctors had found a black spot on Muh's lung. They didn't know at the time whether it was malignant or benign. We knew that it was that dreaded diagnosis: cancer.

Muh had smoked cigarettes for many years. She had stopped smoking fifteen or so years ago. The news of her health problems had led me to make several trips to visit with her. She was always in good spirits. I was considering moving back to Texas so that I could be closer to her during her illness.

Muh had endured many battles that would have killed the average person. She had raised fourteen biological children and seven grandchildren. She had already endured the early loss of three children, Marian, Theo, and C.E. If that wasn't enough, she had many scars from her own childhood that she talked about more often as she grew older.

Muh told me about the painful times when she slept in the woods to avoid my father. She was pregnant during some of those turbulent years. The many years of emotional and physical abuse would have a negative effect on my brothers and sisters, especially those who had witnessed firsthand the abuse.

Muh met my father when she was a young woman. She was in her late teens, and he was in his thirties. She loved him fiercely. While I was growing up, we called him "Mr. West." I did not think about it then, but it was strange that we referred to our biological father as "mister." How distant. How mercurial. In college, I had begun to write a book titled *Mister* or *Blue*. I never completed the manuscript. It was too painful.

There were so many tragedies in my family that I thought that they were normal until many years later. There was so much history that my family kept from me since I was the youngest. I just knew that our family name was stained.

A stained name is a difficult and painful thing, especially during childhood. The violence, death, incarceration, and psychological, emotional, and generational trauma were painful too. I always knew that I wanted to escape the hardships that had befallen so many of my family members.

Amid all this pain, we as a family accomplished much. We were a family that was known to be smart. Some of my sisters had graduated from college and four of my siblings had joined the military. Some of my brothers had the foresight and indefatigable spirit to thrive despite the odds.

East Texas was a difficult place to grow up for African Americans. I often said: "If you can make it out of East Texas, you can make it anywhere." East Texas had a history of lynching and castrating Black men. East Texas was one of the last places to desegregate public schools. It also has one of the highest incarceration rates for Black men in the country.

Many years later, I visited The Legacy Museum: From Enslavement to Mass Incarceration in Montgomery, Alabama. During the tour of the museum, several East Texas counties were on the list of places where Black people were lynched.

As a young man, I was determined to chart a different course. I was grateful to have positive role models from within and outside of my family to support and encourage me. I was surrounded by coaches, schoolteachers, Sunday schoolteachers, neighbors, business owners, and friends who encouraged me.

I was especially close to my basketball coaches. Many of them had taken the time to provide the mentorship and guidance that I so desperately needed. They instilled in me a strong work ethic, both on and off the court.

During the summer months, we "hauled hay," as we called it. We would haul hundreds of square bales and stack them in wooden barns. We were paid .5 cents a bale. It was the primary way that I earned money to buy school clothes from the sixth grade through college.

During my middle school years, my sisters and brothers and I cared for Mr. West at home until he could no longer care for himself. He died during my eighth-grade year. I was with him at the hospital on the day that he died. I didn't know him that well. He tried to make amends for his past sins before he died.

I remember going fishing and hunting with Mr. West as a little boy. I think that he tried to teach me about manhood before he fell ill from a stroke. I will never forget that morning. Mr. West woke up early as normal. This morning something was different. I remember my father calling Muh into the room. I remember him saying that his face and arm were numb. I remember the tears streaming down Muh's face. She knew things would be different now.

Muh quickly massaged his face with moist towels and dressed him while I watched. I knew that something was terribly wrong. Mr. West had suffered a major stroke. He stayed in the hospital for a few days, and then we cared for him at home. Sickness and death seemed omnipresent to us.

When Mr. West died, I felt as if life would spin out of control. I kept the pain within. I knew that for some of my brothers and sisters, the death of Mr. West was a relief. A burden lifted. For me as a young boy, I felt a deep loss for what he was and wasn't.

Mr. West did his best to care for us. I remember his calloused hands getting gifts out of the trunk of his car during Christmas. When thunderstorms would come, he would take the entire family to shelter from the storm in an underground tunnel that he made for us from railroad ties. He tried to shelter us from the storms of life.

I read a poem in my ninth-grade English class that reminded me of my father titled "Those Winter Sundays":

> Sundays too my father got up early
> and put his clothes on in the blueblack cold,
> then with cracked hands that ached
> from labor in the weekday weather made
> banked fires blaze. No one ever thanked him.
> I'd wake and hear the cold splintering, breaking.
> When the rooms were warm, he'd call,
> and slowly I would rise and dress,
> fearing the chronic angers of that house.
> Speaking indifferently to him,
> who had driven out the cold
> and polished my good shoes as well.

> What did I know, what did I know
> of love's austere and lonely offices?
>
> (Robert Hayden, "Those Winter Sundays," from *Collected Poems of Robert Hayden*, edited by Frederick Glaysher. Copyright 1966. Reprinted with the permission of Liveright Publishing Corporation, 1985.)

Muh seemed to have a kind of freedom after Mr. West died. She could finally live out some of her dreams without having to answer to his demands. My brothers and sisters and I were able to help Muh have a new house built on our homestead.

I was proud to be in a position where I could help my mother financially. She had given us so much. It was our time to care and provide for her.

I felt at times that I needed to process all the pain, trauma, and family struggles that had befallen my family. I felt in a sense that I was trying to redeem our family's name and heritage. We all did in our own way.

One of the more tragic stories during my childhood was the story of my brother, Theo. He was absent during most of my childhood. He had been incarcerated in the massive Texas prison system from ages 17-39. Theo had witnessed lots of physical abuse. He had stopped Mr. West from beating Muh too many times. He was seething with anger.

While working in the cotton fields with Muh, Theo had defended her from verbal assaults by the supervisor. Theo had fought with the supervisor to defend Muh. Theo was charged as an adult and would spend most of his life in the Texas prison system. Yet, he was only a child.

I had spent the past decade helping young people who were in the juvenile justice system. Many of them reminded me of Theo. Far too many things had happened to them. Some of them had responded to their pain and trauma by becoming violent themselves.

I would see Theo for the first time when I was in middle school. He died when I finished my senior year in college. He was released from prison and passed away only a few months later.

Another sister, Marian, would die of liver failure due to her alcoholism. She died when I was in seminary in the late 1980s. Many years earlier, she had been so severely beaten by her boyfriend that most of her internal organs were damaged beyond repair. She died in her early forties, and years later, two of her four children died in their early forties.

Many of my brothers, sisters, nieces, and nephews had died in their thirties and forties. I had become all too familiar with death, loss, and grief at an early age.

Another sister, Connie, was pregnant at age fourteen. Connie was an excellent student. While in high school, the principal sexually assaulted her, as did the county constable. Connie was pregnant, allegedly by the high school principal who was White. I heard stories of Mr. West going to the high school to confront the principal. No charges were filed against him. Connie went on to have an abortion, but the pain never left.

Connie struggled with drug addiction much of her life. The principal and the constable were able to keep their jobs despite these horrific acts. Despite her addiction and despite her childhood trauma, Connie eventually became a nurse and won a prestigious award for her accomplishments in nursing.

There was constant conflict in our home. Once, my brother and nephew got into a fight. I was the only one in the house besides the two of them. I tried to separate them so that nobody would be hurt. My brother ran to the back of our house where my father kept his rifles on a gun rack. He came back and aimed the rifle at my nephew's head and pulled the trigger.

I ran down the street to our neighbor's house to call for the ambulance. My heart was racing. I was sure that my nephew was dead. We didn't have a phone at our house. I ran back home, expecting to see my nephew dead only to learn that my nephew had ducked, so that the .22 rifle shot went into the wall just above his head. I was grateful that he hadn't been shot, but I was haunted by the incident.

My brothers would often get into fights and end up in the hospital for treatment. There were too many such incidents to recount. Unfortunately, my sisters were not left unscathed by this. I remember the day that one of my sisters, Wilma, attempted suicide. She was only fifteen or sixteen years old and she had taken several pills. I remember Muh yelling and screaming out of the back door of our house. I knew that something was wrong. Muh would scream out of pain and anguish many times over the years.

The adverse childhood experiences (ACEs) score had not been developed at the time. I just knew that what we were going through wasn't normal. Many years later, I would come to find that we had experienced severe generational trauma. We had also lived with constant toxic stress.

Muh tried to give each of her children and grandchildren the support that they needed. I received support at my home church and from our neighbors. They cared deeply for me. They helped to heal many of my childhood scars.

I was licensed as a Baptist minister at age sixteen. The pastor of our small church and the entire community wrapped themselves around me as I "answered the call" to the gospel ministry. I was beginning to escape the demons that had for too long haunted our family.

I had so many role models who embraced me as a young man. In addition to my mother, brothers, and sisters, our Sunday school teacher, Ms. Reeves, and the Spring Hill Missionary Baptist Church believed in me. She taught me early on how to give speeches before large audiences. I spent hours talking with her about life and how to overcome life's challenges.

While in seventh grade, all the childhood trauma started to catch up with me. I failed seventh grade and had to repeat it. I was testing at a college level, but emotionally, I was a wreck.

I did well during my high school years and had several options to attend college. I chose to attend Austin College, a small liberal arts school a few hours away from Pittsburg. College was a respite from the chaos of childhood. My college coach and the dean of the school and his family were great sources of moral support.

During my college years, I began to find my bearings. I played college basketball and loved the freedom that it provided. I was finally able to live in an environment without the constant trauma of childhood. I was able to live out my dreams and explore my love for literature. I fell in love with Shakespeare, the British Romantics, and Toni Morrison. I was fascinated by her character, Pecola Breedlove. After my college years, I decided to attend seminary at Princeton Theological Seminary in New Jersey. I was fascinated with both politics and ministry.

I knew that I was put on this earth to help alleviate human suffering. I had spent a year of seminary doing ministry at New Jersey State Prison, formerly Trenton State Prison. I had volunteered as a home hospice worker to help people at the end stages of life. I was now working with a national nonprofit organization developing programs to keep young people from being incarcerated.

I learned in my early years that we had to be bearers and transmitters of hope. It was summed up for me in the words of the song "This Little Light of Mine, I'm Gonna Let It Shine." I held on to that song as I traversed life's challenges. It had carried me through many a storm. I was hopeful that it would carry me through the storms that were about to rage.

Muh's Baby Boy

In spite of the hardships, I was grateful for the many people who had been guiding lights in my life. I had worked through a lot of family challenges to try to make a difference in the lives of young people. I felt strongly that the calling in my life was to work with the least, the last, the lost, the lonely and the unloved. In doing so, I was helping to heal some of my childhood wounds.

I had always been a "momma's boy." After the cancer diagnosis, I knew that it was time for me to move back to Texas to be closer to her. I preferred living on the East Coast—but I wanted to be there to help my mother. My sisters did a great job caring for her, but I felt a deep need to provide emotional and financial support for her as well.

After spending a few days with Muh, I drove back to Dallas to catch my flight back to Baltimore the next morning. Lauryn had suggested that I stop by her apartment when I arrived back in Dallas and I was reluctant, but stopped by anyway. She had prepared a meal, and she and I talked for a few hours. After dinner, she started to sing Billie Holiday songs. She said that she was pursuing an acting and singing career and had appeared in some musicals and music videos. It all seemed a bit much, but I listened to her anyway. She liked to talk about herself a lot. She always seemed to embellish her stories.

I noticed that her singing voice wasn't that great, but she had a lot of talent. After singing, I asked her why she had chosen to live in Dallas. She said that she had recently graduated from Tuskegee University and had done an internship at Texas Technology. I found it a bit odd that she was in her late twenties and was just graduating from college. Why was she graduating so late? What had she done in those intervening years?

She was talented. She had a college degree. She was attractive. She had a good job. She had all the right things going for her. Everything seemed great, but something didn't feel right. Maybe my friends' intuition had been right.

Later that night, Lauryn microwaved me a shrimp and pasta dish. I felt that everything was going smoothly. I told Lauryn that I was going to a friend's house. She encouraged me to stay for the night. I decided to stay. The next morning, I had an early flight back to Baltimore. Lauryn made me Pop-Tarts and orange juice for breakfast. I rushed off to the airport. As I departed Texas, I left with a heaviness in my heart about Muh's illness.

Muh was the matriarch of our family. She was the glue that held our family together. I would have done anything to help her through this difficult period.

After arriving back in Baltimore in late July 1999, I felt a deep unease. I had spoken with my sisters Maria and Belinda about Muh's declining health. I spoke with Muh daily on the phone. We were a source of encouragement to one another. She was the center of my universe. She had sacrificed a lot for our family. She deserved to live in peace. She was seventy-four years old. Life had been rough, but she never complained about it. It reminded me of the song that we used to sing at church, "I Won't Complain." She never complained.

I didn't expect that anything would come of my relationship with Lauryn. Everything with her seemed to be staged. I would later come to find that Lauryn had grown up in a troubled family environment as well. She had spent her childhood years living in public housing in both Houston and Chicago. While her parents were married, they suffered from addictions and mental illness that would have painful consequences for Lauryn and her siblings.

Lauryn's father, Bennie, was verbally and physically abusive toward his wife, Beth. She had witnessed many of his drunken episodes when he would beat his wife unmercifully. Bennie often ran the streets and was gone for days at a time. When he returned home, he would repeat the same pattern. Bennie was arrested several times due to his drug addiction. He spent much of his adult life in and out of jail. Beth was left to take care of several children.

Bennie spoke boldly about being a gang member and a hustler. When not in jail or prison, he was chasing other women and drinking and drugging heavily.

Mental illness ran strong on both sides of Lauryn's family. Her father was bipolar. Her mother was paranoid schizophrenic. Lauryn's mother, Beth, attempted to care for her children, but her schizophrenia got the best of her. She often self-medicated by drinking heavily. Lauryn and her siblings grew up without any real supervision in the home. Lauryn was the oldest and cared for her younger siblings as best as she could. Child Protective Services was called into the home on more than one occasion. Lauryn spent some of her early years in and out of foster care or living with neighbors.

Lauryn's mother and father were not able to provide the guidance, structure, and support that Lauryn desperately needed. During one evening after school, one of Lauryn's uncles had waited for her to return home. As she entered the apartment home, she was left alone with her favorite uncle, Uncle John. This time, her Uncle John was not a loving uncle, but a predator waiting to steal her innocence. He sexually assaulted Lauryn from ages seven to nine. Lauryn tried to tell her father what had happened, but he refused to believe her. She refused to tell her brothers out of fear it would cause even further harm. Lauryn suffered in silence. She would carry those scars with her for the rest of her life.

After years of being sexually assaulted by her uncle, Lauryn displayed intense anger and hostility. She once got into a fight with another girl in the community. During the fight, Lauryn bit off the bottom part of a girl's lip. Lauryn ran home with blood all over her face with the girl's lip still in her mouth. She suddenly spat the girl's lip out on the floor. Lauryn was only nine years old.

During her teenage years, the family of one of Lauryn's friends took an interest in caring for her. They saw that she was gifted and talented. The Nelsons had their own challenges, but their family environment was much more stable for Lauryn. The Nelsons were there to help keep Lauryn out of long-term foster care.

The Nelsons had two daughters who were Lauryn's age. Lauryn didn't experience the violence, abuse, and hunger that she dealt with at home. During one of her dates in high school, Lauryn got into an argument with her boyfriend. Her boyfriend struck Lauryn, causing permanent damage to her ability to hear in her left ear.

The Nelsons knew about Lauryn's turbulent family history, but that didn't stop them from caring for her. Lauryn began to exhibit more signs of violence during her high school years. She started to associate with known gang members on the South Side of Chicago. She was searching for her place in the world. She was in pain and didn't have the support and direction that she so desperately needed.

One evening, Lauryn stayed out late. The Nelsons were concerned about her whereabouts. Late that night, Lauryn started banging on the apartment door.

"Please help me," Lauryn yelled as she pounded on the door.

Ms. Nelson finally answered Lauryn's cry for help. Lauryn stood with her arms lifted up and bloody. As her godmother pulled her into the house, Lauryn fell to her knees, crying profusely.

Lauryn yelled, "Damon is dead!"

Damon and Lauryn had left her apartment only a few hours ago. Now Lauryn was screaming that Damon was dead. Had she had something to do with his death? What had happened?

Damon had picked her up from the apartment earlier in the evening. They had gone out to eat. Everything appeared to have been normal then, but they somehow got into an altercation that night that left her boyfriend dead. Lauryn was never convicted of the crime. She had learned at a very early age how to protect herself at any cost.

A few nights earlier, Lauryn had been in an altercation with one of the Nelsons' daughters, Kamesha. The Nelsons had two daughters, Karen and Kamesha. Lauryn had beaten Kamesha so badly that she was bloody and in need of medical attention. The police were called, and Lauryn was taken to juvenile detention. The Nelsons had told Lauryn that she could not return to their home. She had caused too much harm.

Lauryn's violent streak would follow her throughout childhood and into adulthood. Unfortunately, she never received the help that she so desperately needed. Most adults were either afraid of her or avoided her altogether. She was so full of rage that the slightest offense could set her off. The trauma of her early childhood would scar her for the rest of her life.

Lauryn's early victimization would have a negative impact on her siblings as well. Lauryn was the oldest of six children. When her parents were absent, incarcerated, or having difficulty, Lauryn acted as the parent. One evening, Lauryn almost killed her younger brother, Big Mo. She was fifteen years old. Big Mo approached Lauryn while she was asleep. He playfully grabbed her to scare her. They had played like that before.

Later that night, Big Mo was lying on the floor facedown. Lauryn tiptoed toward Big Mo wielding a knife. She slowly approached him and attempted to stab him in the back of the head. Lauryn's younger brother saw her about to stab his big brother and yelled, "Look out, Big Mo!" Big Mo turned to the right just as the knife went deep into the floor. Big Mo would have likely died had Lauryn stabbed him. That was one of many occasions when Lauryn would become uncontrollably violent.

Things would get worse for Lauryn before they got better. She was never going to allow anyone else to victimize her again. She was a ticking time bomb. Everyone around her knew it, yet somehow Lauryn was able to garner the empathy and sympathy of others. She often used this to her advantage.

Lauryn's severe trauma seemed to be causing major problems for her during her late teenage years. She was constantly fighting and in conflict with others. The smallest things could set her off. She would come across as demure and innocent one moment, and raging the next. She was in a constant and perpetual state of rage.

Somehow, Lauryn had pulled it together in spite of her family history. When I met her, she was in her late twenties. At the time, I wasn't aware of the painful events during her childhood and early adult years. I had always wondered if she had been placed in some psychiatric institution or incarcerated. Lauryn was masterful at getting information removed from her record so that nothing negative would appear in a background check.

I would find out many years later that Lauryn had spent many of her young adult years in and out of detention, jail, and psychiatric institutions. Lauryn had helped to kill another young woman who was in an opposing gang. She drove the getaway car. She had dated a known gang leader in Chicago. She would do anything that he told her to do.

Despite such adversity, Lauryn landed a great job at Texas Technology as an engineer in the calculator division. Everything looked good, at least on the surface. Her brilliance, good looks, and chameleon-like qualities opened doors for her.

Through my many years of working with youth, I had found that most kids involved in the juvenile justice or child welfare systems had experienced severe trauma. They had lost a loved one, witnessed violence, or been threatened, bullied, or sexually assaulted. Some of them had been sexually trafficked.

I knew so much about the subject because of my family history and my work. During my childhood, there had been constant chaos. I never liked to use the word "dysfunctional" because of its negative connotations. I liked to say that our family was chaotic. Hardly a week went by in which something tragic didn't happen in our family. Social scientists now know that youth who have experienced a lot of trauma are hypervigilant and often experience a range of symptoms that if untreated can have destructive consequences.

During one of my trips to Texas, Lauryn begged for me to travel with her to Houston. She wanted me to meet her parents. One Sunday, I gave in and rode with her. On the drive to Houston, Lauryn kept discussing her parents' living conditions. She seemed to be embarrassed. Lauryn always dressed in expensive clothing and drove a new SUV. She always lived above her means. Material things gave her a sense of identity and fulfillment.

We finally arrived at Lauryn's parents' apartment. I was a bit nervous. I didn't know what to expect. I walked with Lauryn to her parents' apartment. There were holes in the door as if someone had gotten angry and punched the walls. As I walked in, Lauryn introduced me to her father. He gave me a hug and a handshake as if we had known one another for many years. We traded that manly look that Black men bestow upon one another, both trying to size the other up. I introduced myself. He appeared glad to meet me. I glanced through the apartment and noticed more walls with holes in them. I felt an eerie feeling.

I sat and talked to Lauryn's father for a while. I could tell that he had been drinking heavily. I knew that he had met countless men that Lauryn had brought home over the years.

Lauryn looked a lot like her parents. She acted like her dad. They both were high-energy and seemed to jump from one subject to another. They liked to entertain others even if it meant constantly making up lies.

I met Lauryn's mother, Beth, as well. I could tell that there was a lot of tension between them. Lauryn loved her father but did not have a great relationship with her mother. Lauryn seemed embarrassed about her mother's mental condition. Beth stared into space while her husband did the entertaining.

Lauryn's mother and brother suffered from paranoid schizophrenia. Lauryn's mother looked past me. Lauryn didn't say much to her mother. I could tell that their relationship was either strained or non-existent. With Lauryn's discomfort, we said our goodbyes and left. Her mom walked us to the car. She was holding on to the black metal fence as we were leaving. She was making animal-like sounds while gripping the fence. We quickly left and made the long drive back to Dallas.

Some of the early signs of mental illness that I had begun to see in Lauryn were beginning to make sense. Some things I considered to be very minor would create major disruptions and volatility for her. If I got close to a yellow line on the highway, it would set her off. Basic disagreements would lead her to become threatening. If things didn't go her way, she would take my shoes, shirt, or some other item and refuse to return them to me.

After I met Lauryn's family, I began to wonder if mental illness ran in her family. It became clear that she had some severe psychological and emotional issues.

I would later come to find that she would often make very loud outbursts over very small incidents and then would quickly act as if nothing had occurred.

While riding in the passenger's seat, Lauryn tried to pull the steering wheel on a few occasions. The smallest things would irritate her and cause her to lose control. When these episodes would occur, I would not speak to her for several minutes, and she would calm down. I wanted to process these events, but she would never allow me to discuss these issues with her. She would just act as if nothing had happened.

I once visited Lauryn's apartment. She threatened me because I wanted to leave. When I persisted, she took my bag of clothes and would not give them back to me. I asked her for them several times.

She said, "Leave me the f*** alone, or I will call the f****** police."

Lauryn would often threaten to call the police for very minor things. I left her apartment and returned a few hours later and asked for her to give me my clothes.

After she refused, the police showed up. Lauryn told the police that I was criminally trespassing. Lauryn knew the law better than most police and lawyers. She would always study the law before she did anything crazy so that she could get out of the situation.

After Lauryn called the police, I began to look into her background. I found that she had filed three police reports in Dallas County, Texas. She had filed an assault charge in 1999. Lauryn had reported that she was driving home from a Christian concert when she observed a White male driving up behind her. He was flashing his lights and pulled in front of her and slammed on his brakes. A White male then got out of his truck with a stick in his hand and yelled, "You nigger b****, why don't you go back to Africa where you belong?" He then struck her vehicle several times. As Lauryn exited her vehicle, he kicked her in both legs and grabbed her by her arms and yelled more racial epithets and hit her on the left side of her head with his fists.

Lauryn then reported that the man who had assaulted her got back into his vehicle. She proceeded to follow him while she was on the phone with the police. Lauryn said that she threw a bottle of water through his vehicle window while following him to his residence. When police arrived on the scene, Lauryn was frantic and yelling and screaming about how she had been victimized and called racist slurs. Lauryn did not share how she had burst the windows out of his vehicle and had almost caused the man to wreck his vehicle. She had not attended a Christian concert either. She had filed a false police report, one of many that she would file over the years.

Lauryn was the aggressor, not the person she filed the police report against. Lauryn was great at making things up whenever she saw fit. He would become one of Lauryn's many victims. The entire story was made up. The case was dismissed. Lauryn would get off without incident.

Another police report indicated that Lauryn had an altercation with a man who alleged that she had used a tire tool to knock out the windows of his vehicle. The conflict had started while they were both driving. Somehow, the altercation led to the police being called. They were both parked alongside a major interstate in Dallas. Lauryn was screaming, "Motha f****, you tried to run me off the highway." She then went to the back of her vehicle, took out a tire tool, and proceeded to smash through his front windshield. She did all this while the police were on the phone. This led the other driver to take out his tire tool and shatter her back window.

When the police arrived, Lauryn was crying profusely. Lauryn could cry crocodile tears very easily. It was all an act to her. She played the victim role very well. The police officers sympathized with her and believed her side of the story. They gave the man a ticket. The incident gave Lauryn a sense of entitlement and invincibility. She knew how to manipulate others without any negative consequences. She knew how to survive in the streets of the South Side of Chicago and the low-income housing developments in Houston. She had been in Dallas only a few weeks and she already had crime victims.

Yet another incident occurred at a local gas station near Dallas. Lauryn had attempted to pay for gas and food and did not have enough money to pay for the items. She was very proud and always acted as if she had a lot of money. This led Lauryn to cuss out the store manager. She would use race or whatever she could to get herself out of a bad situation.

"Motha f****, you think that I am stealing," she said.

The manager continued to call the police while she yelled and swore at him. When the police arrived on the scene, Lauryn claimed the store manager had assaulted her. The police wrote a police report, and no charges were filed. Lauryn was allowed to pay the store back for the items.

If nothing else, Lauryn knew how to survive. She was always thinking ahead. She always struck first and then made herself out to be the victim. She could cry at the drop of a dime. She would use sex appeal, if needed, to get things to go her way. I had only known Lauryn for a couple of months. I had picked up signs that she suffered from severe mental illness. All the warning signs were there.

Homecoming

After much thought and prayer, I moved back to Dallas in early October 1999. Muh's health was in decline. I resigned from my job in Maryland and accepted a position as vice president with a non-profit youth-serving agency that I had previously worked for. I was glad to move back home to be closer to family and friends.

A few weeks before my move back to Dallas, Lauryn had told me that she might be pregnant. I had met Lauryn six months earlier. I was overwhelmed, to say the least. I had never planned on having a child without being married.

I didn't think that it was true. When I saw her, she didn't look like she was pregnant, nor did she discuss it. I knew that Lauryn had some severe mental health problems. I was terrified to hear the news.

I had mixed emotions about moving back to Texas. I had lived on the East Coast on and off for seven years. I had lived in Baltimore, Washington, DC, Trenton, Princeton, Cleveland, and New York.

My relationship with Lauryn wasn't serious. Her yelling episodes were too much for me to deal with. After she had called the police on me, supposedly for criminal trespassing, I did not want anything else to do with her. I quickly learned that getting rid of Lauryn would be a challenge of epic proportions.

I had dated a woman named Stacy for many years, but our relationship had waned after my move back to Texas. She had gotten to know my family over the past several years. After I had moved back to Dallas, Lauryn and I had dated periodically. Lauryn had asked me to visit her at her job at Texas Technology. I finally accepted her offer. Once I arrived, she introduced me to several of her colleagues. I didn't feel comfortable. After a few minutes on the premises, I left.

I could tell that she had been making our relationship out to be more than it really was to her co-workers.

Although she was an engineer, she was starting to show signs of major instability. I knew that I could no longer trust her. Yet Lauryn knew how to lure men back into her life. I had begun to see a pattern of behavior. First, Lauryn would do something crazy, like call the police because she was not getting her way. After the incident, she would try and make up for what she had done. She would apologize and attempt to reconcile with sex or gifts. Once Lauryn knew that she was back in your good graces, she would act sane for a few hours, until the next crisis, and the cycle would start all over again.

I had begun to distance myself from Lauryn. Once I moved to Texas, she began to stalk me. She had placed tracking devices on my vehicle. I began to not answer her phone calls. Lauryn kept telling me that she was pregnant, but minutes later would change the story. I did not know what to believe. I had started to keep my distance from her. While leaving my apartment, I noticed her car near my apartment. I was afraid that she would do something to harm me. A few days later, my worst premonitions came true.

I had just arrived at my apartment in the uptown area of Dallas. I had stopped by Sam's Club to buy groceries. As I opened the door to my apartment, Lauryn was standing inside with a tire tool in her hand. Lauryn had only been inside my apartment once before. I had never given her a key to my apartment.

She started yelling expletives. "You Black motha f****. You didn't have to treat me like that."

She struck me with the tire tool several times. I was able to block the blows with my right forearm, then immediately rushed into and locked myself in the bathroom and called the police.

Within minutes, the Dallas Police Department arrived. I showed them the bruises on my arm. Lauryn told the police that she lived with me and that I had been physically abusive toward her. She also told the officer that she was pregnant and that I was the father. We were "common law" according to Lauryn's story. After a brief discussion with his supervisor, Officer Pensky placed Lauryn under arrest. As he attempted to put her arms behind her back, Lauryn began to plead with him not to arrest her.

"I am pregnant with his baby!" Lauryn yelled. "Gerald, please don't let them arrest me. I am carrying your child."

The officer let her know that she did not have a right to assault me. Lauryn was escorted to the police car while pleading with me to drop the charges and to bail her out of jail.

I didn't drop the charges. Someone bailed Lauryn out of jail the next day. After her arrest, she did everything in her power to retaliate against me. She called my cell phone and told me in no uncertain terms, "Motha f****, you owe me $600 for having me arrested. I am pregnant with your baby. Why the f*** did you have me arrested?"

I hung up the phone each time that she called.

After the police had taken her to jail, I began to wonder how she had gotten into my apartment in the first place. I believe that she had told the apartment management that she was my wife, and they had given her a key to my apartment. She also could have entered my apartment while maintenance was there. I would later come to find that Lauryn also knew how to pick locks.

After Lauryn had been arrested, I felt a deep sense of relief. I knew that Lauryn was going to strike again. I also knew that she was angry about her arrest and would retaliate against me. The next day, I left my apartment to travel to Austin on business. When I returned home, I found that my apartment had been broken into. I knew that this was Lauryn retaliating against me for having her arrested. My computer, suits, and some other items had been stolen. I knew that Lauryn had done this or put someone up to it. She knew a lot about computers and technology. I immediately called the Dallas Police Department.

When the police officers arrived, I told them that Lauryn had been released from jail and had most likely broken into my apartment as retaliation for having her arrested. The police tested for fingerprints. They were unable to find any formal evidence to file burglary of a habitation charges against her. I spent the next few nights at a friend's apartment. I knew that she would strike again as soon as she had the opportunity.

I soon realized that Lauryn's goal was blackmail. After several days, Lauryn called and told me she would return my stolen items if I agreed to dismiss the charges against her.

I met with her to get the items back that she had stolen from me at a Pappas restaurant in Richardson, a suburb just north of Dallas. We were in the parking lot. As I approached her vehicle to pick up my stolen goods, Lauryn began to scream, "Motha f****, I'm not giving you s***. I am pregnant with your baby and you had me arrested! F***you."

I immediately got in my SUV. As I attempted to back out of the lot, she pulled up behind me and would not allow me to back up. After several minutes, she moved forward enough to allow me to get out of my parking space. As soon as I started to leave the parking lot again, Lauryn pulled up next to my car and struck the front side of my fender. She was screaming and yelling the entire time. Bystanders started to gather around and watch as she screamed. I immediately called 911 and reported the incident. The 911 operator asked me to stay in the parking lot and wait for the police. My adrenaline was running so high that I left the parking lot and started to head toward downtown Dallas.

Richardson 911 transferred my call to Dallas 911. While I was speaking with the 911 dispatcher there, Lauryn simultaneously called the Dallas Police Department and told them that I had shot at her! Shot at her? I didn't own a gun. This had worked for Lauryn on many past occasions. She would victimize others but would be the first to call the police with her lies and distortions. As both of us were talking to 911, one of the officers who had been involved in her arrest days earlier realized the seriousness of the matter.

The 911 dispatcher kept asking me my location. Lauryn kept following me as I approached the Commerce and Riverfront area of downtown Dallas. Several Dallas Police Department cars arrived at the 1200 Commerce Street location. The police asked Lauryn several times to get out of the vehicle with her hands up. She refused to do so after several commands. After several minutes, the police approached the vehicle, threw her to the ground, and handcuffed her!

Lauryn was arrested on the scene. She did not have a driver's license or insurance. She had outstanding traffic violations and was arrested for burglary of a habitation and stalking. After two arrests and a possible charge of burglary of a habitation, I thought that my history with Lauryn was over. I did not know if she was pregnant or if I was the father of her child. The police had told me that she was seriously mentally ill and that I should cease all contact with her.

I didn't have contact with Lauryn for several days. I was afraid to live in my own apartment. I slept on the couch at my friends' apartments. They were there for me throughout the ordeal. They knew that I didn't have a violent streak in my body. They encouraged me to stay away from Lauryn.

A few weeks later, my friends Reggie and Rob arrived at DFW Airport to pick me up after a trip to Baltimore. Lauryn somehow found out when I was due to arrive at the airport. As I walked out of the terminal, Reggie and Rob pulled up. I placed my bags in their vehicle.

Without warning, Lauryn pulled up and started screaming, "You are not leaving with them. You are going with me."

Lauryn began to strike the hood of Rob's vehicle. She began to cuss at me and my friends. Eventually, the airport police came and asked her to leave. I left the airport with my friends, shaken but not shattered. Once again, Lauryn had evaded an arrest. She seemed impervious to any harm or danger, no matter how extreme her behavior.

Lauryn was tracking my every move. I had once again narrowly escaped. Lauryn knew that she struck fear in others.

Several weeks later, I received a call from Lauryn. She called me from a private number. She said that she was sorry and that she wanted me to sign an affidavit of non-prosecution. I had never heard of an affidavit of non-prosecution before. She told me that it was a way to drop the charges so that they would not appear on her record and affect her employment. I discussed this with some lawyer friends. They both encouraged me not to sign the affidavit.

A few days later, I met Lauryn at the Dallas Police Department. Lauryn had set up a meeting with an officer to discuss the affidavit of non-prosecution. The officer with her was a Black female. The officer pleaded with me not to drop the charges.

The officer told me, "Sir, I have seen this time and time again. The charges are dropped, but the violence does not end. This woman has some serious issues. Just let the process work itself out in the courts."

I told the officer that I would think about it, but I would likely drop the charges. I told her that I did not want to affect her employment. I signed the affidavit of non-prosecution. I would live to regret it.

Calm Before the Storm

I didn't have any contact with Lauryn for a few months after I had signed the affidavit of non-prosecution. I had hoped that signing it would permanently stop Lauryn from harassing me. I still didn't know if she was pregnant. I knew that she was vindictive and would do anything to get back at me for having her arrested.

My life had begun to get back to normal. I had met Lauryn just six months earlier and it had been a whirlwind. I finally started to have the kind of peace that I was accustomed to. My job was going well. I was enjoying life in Dallas. I had found a progressive church that I attended. Things were coming together rather nicely. I knew that calm often comes before the storm with Lauryn.

Months prior, I had met a friend of Lauryn's at Club GiGi's in Dallas. She told me to watch my back.

"She is obsessed with you. She has pictures of you and stabs your picture on the kitchen table. She is crazy as hell. That b**** is crazy!"

After Lauryn's former roommate told me to "watch my back," I was extremely cautious.

Just a few days later, I received a call from a Dallas Police Department detective who told me that Lauryn had brought phone harassment charges against me for a verbal dispute. On the date that Lauryn alleged that we had a verbal dispute, my office had been broken into. I knew that Lauryn was the culprit. The detective said that the charges were being dismissed due to a lack of evidence and history.

One Sunday afternoon in early February 2000, I received an urgent call from one of my sisters. I knew that something had gone terribly wrong. She said that Muh was lying in bed but couldn't move. They told me to hurry home. I quickly jumped into my vehicle and drove to Pittsburg. Pittsburg was 120 miles east of Dallas. I made it in a little more than an hour. I hoped and prayed for the best but expected the worst.

Tears were streaming down my face as I entered the room to see Muh lying on her bed. I feared that she had suffered a stroke. She had a huge smile on her face as always, but she couldn't talk. She couldn't move most of her body. She could move her face, but the rest of her body was paralyzed. We rushed her to the hospital. This was the scariest day of our lives. Our family matriarch was not invincible this time. She had overcome so much. She had always rebounded. I was afraid that things were more serious this time around.

After a few hours of observation, the hospital moved Muh to Mother Francis Hospital in Tyler, Texas. They provided better care for her and had much better medical facilities. The doctors quickly determined that the lung cancer had metastasized to her brain. The cancer had caused some of the paralysis. I could tell from the medical doctors' statements that the prognosis didn't look good.

Muh had rebounded well from a past surgery to remove cancer from her intestines. I knew that she was a fighter and survivor.

I picked up my mother's only living sister, Aunt Gail, and took her to see her baby sister. A day later, the doctors gave us two options: give Muh brain surgery that could cause her to lose most of her functionality or allow her to live as long as she could and let the disease take its natural course. After a discussion with the family, we chose the latter. Muh died the next day. It was the darkest and cruelest day of our lives.

Our entire family was devastated. I was numb. It had been a hellish few months and now Muh had died. She had been the wind beneath my wings. We all gathered at the family homestead and shared memories. We were all beside ourselves. Lauryn had heard about my mother's passing. I don't know how, but Lauryn always had a way of just knowing things.

Muh's funeral was held a week later at our home church. There was an outpouring of support from the local community. Several of my friends from other cities and states arrived to show their support.

As we were about to proceed to the church for the funeral service, Lauryn showed up. My family knew about the crazy things that she had done to me. One of my sisters carried a pistol and wanted to use it on her, but I encouraged her to put it away. My past girlfriend, Stacy, showed up at the funeral as well. We had dated for several years, and she was loved and respected by my family.

As the funeral service proceeded, Lauryn went to the podium and told them how much she loved my mother. She had only met her once at the hospital in Tyler. During her visit, Muh had said that there was something wrong with her. I should have listened. My family members had discouraged me from dating her.

Lauryn was wearing maternity clothes so that everyone would know that she was pregnant. She told the audience that she was carrying my child. I was devastated. Stacy also made a few remarks about my mother. I was embarrassed by the entire scene. Lauryn had not been invited to the funeral. Somehow, we made it through the funeral without incident.

Two days after the funeral, I returned to work. I was still in shock. I had a lot of grieving to do. I arrived back at my office, located on Martin Luther King, Jr. Boulevard in Dallas. I did not take any time off from work. I also didn't want to think about my mother's death. Lauryn knew that I was vulnerable. She was upset that Stacy had shown up at the funeral.

I was sitting in my office upstairs on a Monday just two days after the funeral. I received a knock on the door. There were two Dallas police officers at my door.

They asked, "Are you Gerald Ingram?"

I nervously said, "Yes."

The officers then surrounded me and placed my arms behind my back and said, "You are under arrest!"

They handcuffed me and took me past my staff at the office and placed me in a police car waiting downstairs. The handcuffs felt like razors on my wrists. All kinds of thoughts raced through my head. Why me? What did I do to be arrested? Why is this all happening now?

My heart seemed to jump out of my chest. My mind was racing. How could this happen? I had signed two affidavits of non-prosecution just a few months earlier. I was the victim. I hadn't done anything illegal. She was required to attend batterers' intervention groups. How could the tables have turned so quickly? How could I so quickly have gone from a victim of two crimes to being considered a perpetrator? I was arraigned that night on a misdemeanor phone harassment charge. I was bonded out and released that night.

Once released, I went to my apartment and called family and friends. They were genuinely concerned for my safety once again. I lived in the same apartment that Lauryn had burglarized just a few months earlier. I knew that Lauryn would go to any length to retaliate. She and I had no communication with one another for months. How could I be charged with phone harassment when we had no contact?

To make things worse, my employer had received a call from a person identifying themselves as a law enforcement officer in Dallas, Texas. The person calling was a female and spoke to the then vice-president of operations, Mary Bowers. The woman calling referenced my name and said that I had been arrested for abusive behavior. She would not leave her name. Years later, I would come to find that Lauryn had called my employer acting as a Dallas law enforcement representative. Lauryn would often act out different characters. This time it was acting like a detective. At other times, she would act like Barney, the purple dinosaur, or revert to acting like a child. She would pose as many different people as the years went by. I always wondered if she also suffered from dissociative identity disorder, previously called multiple personality disorder.

I settled back into my work the next day. I didn't feel comfortable after I had been arrested at my place of employment. The following day, I received another knock on my office door. They called out my name as I approached the door.

"Are you Gerald Ingram?"

"Yes," I responded.

"You are under arrest for a terroristic threat."

This time, I almost fell from the shock of the officer's words. Terroristic threat? I hadn't threatened anybody. Once again, I hadn't even communicated with Lauryn.

The officers handcuffed me and took me back to jail for the second time in two days. I was trying to grieve from the greatest loss in my life. Instead, Lauryn was trying to put me away for good. She knew that I had political ambitions. She wanted to destroy me for having called the police twice against her. I had tried to resolve things amicably by signing the affidavits of non-prosecution.

I was arraigned a second time within two days. The judge presiding over the arrangement was Judge Candace Carl. The clerk called my name to approach the bench. Judge Carl asked me if I was the same person who had appeared before her in court two nights ago on phone harassment charges. I told her that I was the same person.

She then asked, "How do you plead?"

I stated, "Not guilty."

After my statement, I asked the judge if I could ask her a question. She agreed.

I asked her, "How could I be arrested twice on charges that never happened?"

Judge Carl looked palpably upset. She hit the gavel and said, "Your bail is set at $250,000. If you say another word, I will raise it to a million dollars."

At that moment, a guy on the bench beside me whispered, "Shut up, nig***. This judge will raise your bail to a million dollars."

I sat back on the bench with my mind swirling. How could I be in this position? Why me? How could the system work like this?

I sat back on the bench and watched as other men were arraigned. Most of the men were either Black or Latino. One man was arraigned on murder charges. His bail was set at $100,000. I had never been to jail in my adult life. I knew how the juvenile justice system worked. I had been helping young people to successfully complete probation and prevent further involvement in that system. This was my first personal contact with the adult criminal justice system. I had worked all my life to be an upstanding citizen and help others avoid incarceration. Now I was facing serious charges!

I knew that there were major inequities in the criminal justice system. I knew that the mass incarceration of Black men was real. Dallas County had a sordid history of incarcerating Black men at alarming rates. Dallas was one of many Southern cities that had a White Citizen's Council, which acted with impunity against Black people. Dallas's district attorney at the time, Bill Hill, was a chief proponent of mass incarceration. Three of my brothers had done time in the Texas prison system. I knew how harsh the system could be. I had spent almost a decade of my life trying to reform the juvenile system, and now I was caught up in the same criminal justice system that I had helped countless young people to avoid.

After the arraignment, my bail was set at $250,000. My bail was set higher than men who had been arraigned on murder charges!

My attorney at the time suggested that we have a bail-reduction hearing. Posting $250,000 to get out of jail with no assurances that the money would be returned was a steep hill to climb. My private investigator at the time, Candi Collins, worked tirelessly to ensure that I was released from the Dallas County jail as quickly as possible.

Candi visited me in jail and told me the news that we had to wait up to ten days for a bail-reduction hearing. I was devastated. When she told me the news, I struck the plexiglass and began to weep. I was in disbelief. I was still grieving the loss of Muh.

I read one book a day to keep from losing my mind. Books had always been my escape during childhood. I would read encyclopedias that Muh brought home from her cleaning jobs.

I didn't want to interact with the guys in my jail cell. They left me alone and referred to me as "old school." I had heard horror stories about what happened to men in jail. I had stayed in Dallas County jail for ten days for a crime I did not commit. I didn't think that I would make it. I witnessed constant fighting between Black and Hispanic jail inmates. They had nothing to lose. It was a war inside the jail system. I stood out like a sore thumb. They couldn't figure out how I ended up in the system. I didn't look or talk the part. I told them the story of how I ended up getting arrested, but they didn't believe me. It all seemed surreal.

After my second arrest, the bail-bond-reduction hearing couldn't come soon enough. My attorney and private investigator had contacted several friends and colleagues to appear during the hearing. I appeared in court in an orange jumpsuit. The jumpsuit was made for someone six feet tall, not six feet, seven inches tall.

Finally, the day arrived for the bail-reduction hearing. Lauryn showed up in rare fashion. She looked as demure and innocent as possible. She carried a briefcase and stood between two female prosecutors. She glanced at me in the jumpsuit with a twinkle in her eye. She had me where she wanted me. She knew that she had the upper hand. In less than thirty days, I had lost my mother and been arrested twice. I was beside myself.

Sitting behind Lauryn on the bench was a young Black woman. I didn't know at the time if she was Lauryn's relative or if she had something to do with the hearing. Through my attorney, I found out that her name was Patricia. She worked with Lauryn at Texas Technology. Allegedly, she had heard me threaten Lauryn while at work.

The presiding judge finally called the hearing to order. I testified about my employment and how all the affidavits filed by Lauryn were untrue. Several community members who knew my reputation were there to support me as well. While Lauryn was on the stand, she stated how fearful she was of me. My attorney cross-examined her about her previous arrests. He made the case that Lauryn was being retaliatory.

While Lauryn was on the stand, the presiding judge asked Lauryn a question, and she raised her voice at the judge. The judge was visibly upset with her lack of control. A few minutes later, the judge ordered that I be released from jail and that my bail be lowered to $500.

In a matter of hours, Lauryn had threatened the court reporter and yelled at the presiding judge. The stenographer shook her head at Lauryn's inappropriate behavior. Many years later—thirteen to be exact—the same stenographer would be present at another court hearing involving Lauryn and me. I quickly thanked my friends for being there to support me and went back to jail for a few hours until

I was released. These had been the ten most challenging days of my life. There were major storm clouds ahead, but at least I was about to get my freedom back.

The day after I was released from jail, Lauryn called me from a private number on my cell phone. She was crying profusely.

"I'm sorry. I'm sorry," she kept saying over and over. "I know that I can get in trouble calling you. I am several months pregnant. What do I need to do to get you out of this? I gave my life to the Lord. I could not see straight. I was so hurt at the funeral. I was embarrassed. At some point, we will have to talk. She will be here soon, our daughter that we made together. They know that you are the father of my child. Can you forgive me? I don't know the case number for the misdemeanor charge, but I dropped the charges. I want you to be happy. I actually wanted a boy."

I hung up the phone!

It seemed like an eternity had gone by since my mother had passed away. I had been arrested twice within two days on trumped-up charges.

Lauryn was an expert at knowing how to work the criminal justice system to her advantage. She didn't mind using sexual favors to get what she wanted. After my two arrests, I discovered that Lauryn had filed false affidavits against me dating back to January 14, 2000. She had worked closely with the district attorney's office to gain their sympathy. Two of the prosecutors in the family violence division of the Dallas district attorney's office worked to help Lauryn at any cost.

Through discovery, I was able to read one of the false affidavits that Lauryn had filed against me. Lauryn wrote the following in her affidavit filed on January 14, 2000:

> I am Lauryn Burns, Product Development Manager for Texas Technology for three years. Today I am here to file charges against my ex-boyfriend Gerald Ingram. The reasons are as follows: The evening of January 5, 2000, between the hours of 10:30 p.m.–11:30 p.m., Gerald had phoned me while on the phone. I

asked if I could call him back later. Within ten minutes, I returned his call to knowingly focus on our unborn child. Immediately, Gerald began yelling at me for not returning his call over the previous two days. I had tried to explain that I had been extremely busy with work and did not mean to upset him. He continued to yell at me, so I hung up on him. I became terrified as to what he might do if I did not call him back immediately, therefore I did call him back within seconds. Again, he yelled at me, "Stupid b**** you have one more time to hang up on me and that's you're a**." There was a moment of silence, then he said, "Let's talk about something else." I began talking and jumped right into the topic of abortions. I had mentioned to him that I could not cover the finances of an abortion and that if I terminated the pregnancy, I would be facing serious health issues. The two main health issues that I revealed to him were that I had non-cancerous fibroid cysts on my uterus, which could cause severe internal bleeding should an abortion procedure be performed. The other issue was that I've been medically advised that due to the size of my fibroid cysts (total of four), if I were to have an abortion, there would be a strong possibility of me not being able to bear children in the future.

    I went on to tell Gerald that we might want to consider surgery as a method of removing the unborn child. Although I am truly against abortions but pro-choice for others, I could not envision myself being tied to this man the rest of my life. As the conversation continued, with no direct solution other than for me to have the baby (I am a little over three months pregnant), I grew tired of talking to Gerald and asked that we not talk anymore until the baby is born. At this point, Gerald, as usual, began asking me to marry him and went on about how much he loved me. My response to his comments was, "After all of the physical/verbal abuse, lies, deception, and false reports, leading to defamation of character, there is absolutely no way now or in the future I will consider marrying you or entertain another relationship with you. I'm sorry, Gerald, it's over between you and me." Again, Gerald ignored all I had stated and said, "Lauryn, I know I messed up and have hit you and lied about you to the police, but I will show you how much I have changed. I promise I will make things right between us." I replied, "Gerald, stop it. Now I'm ready to go to bed and from here on out take care of yourself. I hope you seek professional help for your problems. I just can't do this anymore. I have to focus my energy on the fact that I am going to be a mother and I don't need any additional stress. I'm already having a complicated pregnancy."

Gerald immediately cut me off and in his exact words said, "b****, do you think this is a f****** game?" I cut in by saying, "Gerald, no I don't, but I am afraid of you, please…" Gerald cut me off again and said, "Lauryn, you think I'm bullsh****** You know what they say: if I can't have you, no one else will. Lauryn, I will kill you first." Immediately I grabbed a piece of paper and began jotting down everything he was saying to me. I was trying to write down everything, yet I did not catch all of the profanity he called me in the midst of trying to write down his comments. Within 30 seconds, I said to Gerald, "I am going to file a protective order against you." Although my voice was shaking, I tried hard not to show any fear, but I was unsuccessful. I truly am afraid for my life. In response to my saying that I would file a protective order, Gerald said, after laughing uncontrollably, "I'm convinced you are one dumb b****."

Why do you think I filed so many false reports against you? Because I know that no one would listen to you. They are not going to grant you a protective order against me. I'm a leader for my job and I know people in high places and they aren't going to do a f****** thing to me. One of these days, and real soon, I'm going to catch you off guard again and this time I'm going to snatch your skinny little ass up in some bushes, stick my hand up your p**** and kill you and the f****** baby! Lauryn, this is not a threat, it's a promise. Don't f*** with me. I'm gonna blow your f****** brains out. I'll see to it that you and the baby are six feet underground before I let you out of my life, so watch your back. As I sat there in this room, tears started running down my face, for I knew that my days were numbered on this earth. What did I do in this life to deserve my life being taken away? I have enrolled in the Family Violence Program for help and even considered staying in a shelter. I fear for my life and that of my unborn child. As I write this report, I know in my heart that there is no turning back now. But someone has to know that when Gerald does kill me, at least it will be on paper. Before I continue with the evening of January 5th conversation, please tell my family that I loved them dearly. It wasn't their fault. I just ended up choosing an ill-minded man and there is absolutely no way out this time around.

You know, I held on to the telephone with shaking hands, listening and writing everything down he was saying. I knew that after repeatedly telling Gerald that I wanted no part of a relationship with him anymore that he felt he'd reached a dead end and the consistent incongruity of a relationship was over. He felt that this was the last straw. I responded to Gerald by saying, "Maria James is one of my attorneys and I'm going to pursue a protective order for you to stay away from me as many times as needed. I don't care how many times the judge may possibly turn me down for a protective order, my blood will be in the hands of the law and I have faith that someone, somewhere, will listen. I'd rather die if it meant being with you. I'd rather die if it meant giving up all that I have worked for. I'd rather die than submit my soul to you, Gerald. I'd rather die." I hung up the phone and took it off the hook. I ran in my room, locking my bedroom door, since Shirley, my roommate, was over at her boyfriend Larry's house. I slept in my bed with a bottle of mace in my hand. All night I tossed and turned. At 4:00 a.m. I sat up in the living room awaiting daylight and praying that Gerald would not kick in my door. On the morning of January 6, I phoned the police, which brings me to this point of asking for help. I do not want to die—please help me! Please! Please! Please! Gerald is going to kill me, and I have nowhere to run and hide. He called me at work the very next day but I hung up on him. I know he's watching my every move. He's going to kill me; please hear my cry, please! Humbly submitted, Lauryn. January 14th, 2000.

This was just the beginning of Lauryn making up false affidavits and getting the police, district attorney's office, judges, attorneys, and many other officials to believe her. I thought that the district attorney's office would see through her charade, but miraculously, they did not. I would later find that, while under Bill Hill, the Dallas district attorney's office was more consumed with getting convictions than getting justice.

Lauryn and I had never discussed having an abortion. Lauryn's fantasies would get more severe as the years went by.

I had a new legal team that was very aggressive. My legal team worked vigorously on the charges that I was facing. The private investigator asked me several questions about Lauryn. After several weeks of investigation, he was not able to find anything substantial in Lauryn's background.

Years later, I found that Lauryn had an extremely violent history. In addition to her relationships with gang members, Lauryn had a proclivity for acting out violently. Once, Lauryn had an altercation at a fast-food restaurant. Lauryn was in the drive-through. She had ordered a burger and fries. She was unhappy with how her burger had been prepared. Lauryn immediately got out of the drive-through, walked to the front of the line, and yelled, "Who f***** up my burger?" A woman was attempting to answer her question when Lauryn lost control and jumped over the counter, picked up a vat of hot grease, and threw it on the face and body of the woman who had offended her. The woman had serious burns all over her body. She almost died due to her severe burns.

Lauryn ran out of the restaurant and was later arrested. She was somehow able to get the entire incident removed from her record. Lauryn's sister informed me that she had spent a few months in jail and then in a psychiatric hospital for the incident. Lauryn had basically crippled an innocent woman who didn't fix her burger to her liking. She was able to get out of the situation unscathed.

I often wondered how Lauryn was able to manipulate the criminal justice system. How was she able to harm so many people and still not have a criminal record?

Lauryn was extremely impulsive. Any small thing could set her off at any moment. There were many other times when Lauryn ran people off the highway because of road rage. She used her vehicle as a lethal weapon.

Lauryn was a survivor. She knew how to navigate and negotiate the harsh streets of Chicago, Houston, and now Dallas. She knew how to wear expensive clothing and act like she was a business professional. She also knew how to be violent and live life as a gangster. She knew how to "code switch," as Elijah Anderson would say. She had made the system work for her, even though she was the one committing the crimes. It would catch up with her, eventually.

Free at Last

After I was released from jail, I felt a deep sense of relief. I had spent ten days in jail for crimes I didn't commit. I was also deeply depressed. Instead of grieving about my mother's loss, I was fighting for my very life. I was baffled that any person could so easily manipulate the legal system.

I was encouraged by the outpouring of support. My job was solidly behind me. Mary Bowers, Tim Johnson, and John Fisher were constant sources of support. My brothers and sisters supported me as well. They knew that this was not part of my character. My therapist at the time told me that I was dealing with situational depression and post-traumatic stress disorder. I was taking medication, but it was not helping. I was also drinking heavily at the time.

I saw my counselor, Steve, for therapy every week. We talked about my present situation as well as my childhood. Steve was politically connected and helped me meet with key government officials who could help me get justice. Steve facilitated a meeting with the Dallas County Sheriff. The sheriff expressed support and assured me that he would do his best to help with the case. Steve and I also met with a deputy police chief at the Dallas Police Department.

I remained grounded in my faith. I was a preacher and knew something about faith, but I had never been under this kind of attack. I had been attending St. Luke Community United Methodist Church. The pastor, Zan Holmes, was a great preacher and social justice advocate. I would attend on Sundays to renew and revive my soul. Everything that I had worked for was falling apart. I had gone from East Texas to elite schools, but that didn't matter now. I was just another Black man caught up in the criminal justice system.

I poured myself into my work. When I wasn't working, I was drinking. On Sunday nights, I was with friends at the club, GiGi's. One Sunday, I saw Patricia at the club. She had attended court with Lauryn and worked with her at Texas Technology. I tried to approach her, but she was reluctant. My friend Mark knew her. She let Mark know that Lauryn was crazy and the best thing that I could do was to leave Dallas.

My attorneys were hard at work getting the charges dismissed. I felt that my legal team would be able to clear my name. One strategy that they employed was to depose Patricia. After several weeks, my legal team was able to conduct the deposition. That would help to turn the case around. My attorney took the lead in questioning Patricia:

"Patricia, how long have you known Lauryn?"
"A few months."
"How long are a few months?"
"Like, three or four months."
"Are y'all friends or do you hang out outside Texas Technology?"
"Not really."
"What does 'not really' mean?"
"I have seen her at a club called GiGi's before."
"Where is that club located?"
"Dallas."
"So, do you know Gerald?"
"Not really."
"What do you mean, not really?"
"I heard his voice before."
"Have you ever heard Gerald's voice before today?"
"Yes."
"So, you are here today because you heard Gerald threaten Lauryn, correct?"
"Yes."
"Did you hear an argument going on between them? Do you remember?"

"Yes, she was just saying what was going on between them because she was talking to the receptionist about how their relationship was."

"What was going on at that point? Do you remember?"

"I don't know. Like, he was beating her up or something. I don't know what she was talking about. I really wasn't paying too much attention to her. She was just talking about some crap. I hope I can say that."

"You can say anything you want to—as long as it's the truth. Good, bad, or ugly. So, then you met her at the funeral?"

"No, I didn't see her at the funeral. He met her the day of the funeral."

"The funeral was in Mt. Pleasant or something, right?"

"Right," said Patricia. "She was saying that she was gonna go to the funeral and buy some clothes, then get her hair done, and all this good stuff. It was, like, two days before. I think she got there early that day."

"How come she's showing you her hair and nails? She doesn't even know you."

"I know. She is really friendly. She needs a friend or something."

"She needs a friend, so she latched on to you?"

"Yeah, I guess. I'm just that type of person."

"Okay."

"She was supposed to show me her hair but didn't because I had a half-day at work. I think I had to go to the doctor's office or something."

"Are you taking mood-altering pills like tranquilizers or anything?"

"No, I am not. I was taking diet pills at the time."

"Okay, thank you. You're tough."

"But my doctor took me off them because I wasn't taking them right or something. And that makes me upset because he took me off my diet pills, but I'm not gonna cry on camera. If he'd only given me another week… Anyways, the reason I knew about the funeral is because she sent me an e-mail."

"From Gerald?"

"Not from Gerald, but she had gotten into his AOL account."

"Gerald's AOL? She showed you where she had broken into his AOL account?"

"Yeah. He had called her earlier that morning, and she was saying, I bet his ex-girlfriend is going to be there."

"He had called her that morning, and she decided to go check his AOL account?"

"Yeah, to tell her exactly where he was gonna be and that his mom had passed away. She broke into his account and found out exactly where he was gonna be, and she was asking me, 'Well, do you think he's gonna be here?' I was like, I don't know where he was supposed to go. So, I don't know. I don't understand."

"How did she get into his account? Did she tell you?"

"I think he's stupid if you just ask me. I think he's stupid because one, I told him…and I told him, 'Listen…' Because I met Mark at the club and I was drunk, and I shouldn't have, but I couldn't care less. I said, 'Listen, you're stupid. The girl's got your cell phone number, she's got your address, and the stupid girl's got your AOL.' Did he listen to me? No, he didn't listen to me. He thought that I was lying. He's stupid, a loser."

"He'll enjoy that."

"I hope he watches this—loser!"

"Okay, right before the funeral, she said, 'Come look at this, I'm in his mail.'"

"What did you see?"

"She showed me a picture that she had saved on her computer—a picture of his ex-girlfriend and a letter that he never received because she had erased them because they were from his ex-girlfriend that stays in Virginia, I think. There was a whole bunch of things that she showed me, and I was like 'Dang, how you do that?' I guess she just kind of looked over his shoulder and found out a way. And then she was telling me about how he came up to her house and they got into an argument and she called the police. She was saying that he didn't want her to come to the funeral."

"Did she tell you what she did at the house when she called the police?"

"I don't know what she was saying. I think she was just saying stuff about arguing."

"And she called the police. But didn't she say that he hit her too, or he beat her up or assaulted her?"

"No, I think he was probably trying to leave. I'm not for sure."

"You got a good memory. Keep going."

"Okay, and when she got back, she was saying how much he was with the ex-girlfriend, and she was upset because his ex-girlfriend stood up with him when the pastor said, 'All the parents…' No, the pastor said, 'All the children, just stay there, and the couples just stand up.'"

"And the ex-girlfriend stood up with him?"

"Yeah. And she was upset about that."

"And she was there."

"Yeah. And nobody knew she was pregnant. Then she was telling me about how the girl came back from Virginia and stayed with him. So, she was upset about that, and she called the police."

"Why? Because the ex-girlfriend was there?"

"Yes, just because the ex-girlfriend was there, and she kind of got those charges back. So, then she said that he was in jail, but they were still keeping in contact because she was checking his mail."

"While he was in jail and stuff?"

"Yeah, she was checking his mail while he was in jail. When he got out of jail, she was telling me how upset he was. I felt sorry for her, being pregnant and all. So, I had some fruit, and I went over and told her, 'Hey, if you want something to eat, there's some fruit over there or something.' Then, she was like, 'Come here, come here. He told me he was going to kill me for putting him in jail.' I was like, 'Well, I think you should call the police.' She was like, I have a restraining order on him, and it's supposed to be coming in right now."

"What's supposed to be coming in right now?"

"The restraining order."

"Okay, this is really important. Let's go slow. There was a day where you were going to be nice and take her some fruit. Did you take the fruit into her office? Does she have a cubicle?"

"Yeah, she has a cubicle. I didn't take the fruit into her office."

"Okay. What did you do?"

"I just went around the corner where her cubicle was and asked her if she wanted anything. There was some fruit over there."

"Okay, so you told her, 'There's some fruit. Come on over here and get some if you want.'"

"Yes."

"At this point, she said, 'Come here. I want to talk to you.'"

"Yes."

"And you walked into her cubicle and…what happened then?"

"And then she said, 'Listen to this.' And you can turn up your phone real loud. Now, I am not sure it was him. I don't know who it was. I don't know if that person was saying anything. The only thing that I know is that she was like, 'Oh, you're gonna kill me?' She was repeating this. So, I don't know if there was anybody on the phone. That's my thing. I don't know nothing. I just don't know what was coming out of her mouth."

"So, you couldn't even hear a voice on the phone. You don't know if there was a person there or not?"

"Not at all."

"And if there was a person there, you don't know who it was?"

"Right"

"Okay, she was then saying, 'You're gonna kill me? Is this what you're gonna do?'"

"Yeah."

"Then there was nothing."

"There was nothing. Then she was like, 'You're gonna kill me for putting you in jail?' Some crap she was saying. So, I was like, 'You need to call the police. He threatened you. You need to call the police.' So, she calls the police. She even goes to talk to them. At this time, I'm kind of upset with Lauryn."

"Just call it like it is, that's all. Now, that's real important. For Gerald or against Gerald. For Lauryn or against her."

"I don't care about either one of them."

"There was an old movie that said, 'Just the facts, ma'am, nothing but the facts.'"

"Okay, 'cause I could care less about either one of them. My twenty-second birthday just passed, and these people are bothering me."

"Happy birthday."

"So, we go downstairs, we call the police, and the police tell her to come on-site. So, she ends up running upstairs and getting a paper…"

"Getting what paper?"

"Getting a paper about the twenty-four hours."

"Yes."

"So, then she ends up talking to a detective. The detectives talk to her and make sure, you know, the police can get on the site, and I had other business to take care of, so I left."

"Did you talk to the police?"

"Not at all. They couldn't care less what I had to say."

"Well, you didn't have anything to say. You didn't hear anything. You just heard her talking? Did you hear anything about a baby or killing a baby?"

"Did you know she told me something about that?"

"When? After…maybe a day later?"

"I think it was before that."

"Before that?"

"I think it was before that. I think he was gonna, like, stick his hand inside her and pull the baby out or something like that."

"But you never heard anything like that, right?"

"No, I didn't hear that. That's what she had told me, and I was like, 'That's kind of sick.'"

"Okay, that's pretty far out, for sure. So, it wasn't your idea to tell her to do that?"

"No."

"Did anybody else tell her that was a good idea to tell that story that you know of? Did she talk to anybody else? Who else did she talk to up there?"

"Up there? Nobody, because everybody up there, as far as I know… Well, after the fact, after I met the girl, people were telling me to leave her alone. She's crazy about this man."

"She's crazy over him, but that doesn't make her crazy, probably. She's crazy, or she's just in love?"

"Obsessed. That would be a very good word. She's obsessed. It's just like, Gerald, Gerald, Gerald."

"Obsessed."

"Yes. She told me that later on. After that, I met Mark at the club. This was after I went to the court thing."

"Let's talk about that. She obviously said, I want you to come to court. And I want you to tell the story that he said he was going to kill me and yank my baby out and all that stuff on the stand."

"She didn't say, 'Yank the baby out?'"

"Okay. What did she say on the stand in court?"

"In court, she really didn't say too much of nothing."

"What were you going to say? What were you gonna have to testify to?"

"I didn't have the slightest idea what I was gonna have to testify to."

"Did you talk to an attorney or the district attorney's office before you went there?"

"I talked to a lady, and she was saying, 'What did you hear?' And I told her what I heard and whom I heard it from."

"Did you tell the lady you heard Gerald say it?"

"No."

"But if you did, you were mistaken?"

"Then I was mistaken."

"You're absolutely sure you never heard it. You are not changing your story because…I'm gonna be a mean guy for a minute."

"Okay, be a mean guy."

"This is gonna come, probably before long, that you'll be sworn in your testimony. This is a big deal. You're a big witness. It's perjury. Don't lie for Gerald. Don't lie for Lauryn. Just tell the truth. You absolutely had no idea even if there was anybody else on the telephone?"

"I'm absolutely, positively sure."

"Is she capable of making up something like that?"

"I believe so. In my mind, I believe so. I really, really, really do. I want to call her…"

"Call her what it is."

"The b**** is a psycho. Because one, she wanted to—she asked me if she could or if I would, and the b**** don't even know me."

"No, ma'am, I don't."

"No, I am talking about her. She doesn't know me. Not too many people know me, and there's not too many people that I hang around with. I'm kind of the type of person that stays to myself, really, because people kind of irk me when they get on my nerves, and there's not too many people that I trust. But she asked me if it were possible…and she would pay me, and this would be true…and my mother's gonna get…and wonder why I was talking to this man, but I couldn't give a flip—and she asked me about going to Virginia with her to go and get this girl."

"Go get her? To buy her some new clothes?"

"No, no, no. I'm gonna tell you. She said that when she was younger and she was about my age, she was working with this girl, and she was working with this old lady like me and her, real cool or whatever, and that the girl had a boyfriend, or a baby daddy, or whatever, and the girl waited up, and the girl was real, real upset. I guess the boyfriend had a new girlfriend or something, and the girl shot the woman dead, and she [Lauryn] drove the car…the getaway car. So, she expected me to be her when she was younger. Because she was the one driving the getaway car, she expects me to drive the getaway car. She said she would just tell him that we were going out for vacation, and she'd talk to my boss and tell him I was sick or something so we could get out."

"So, she was gonna make up another story to be her alibi to go out and…"

"To Virginia and shoot this girl. Shoot her, beat her up, something, but I was supposed to drive the getaway car. One, I'm not stupid. Two, I'm not stupid."

"Was she gonna pay you?"

"She said she was gonna pay me."

"She didn't have some love thing toward her or you, did she? I know that's an off-the-wall question."

"Are you saying did I have sex with her?"

"No, no, no. I didn't go that far."

"No, I haven't, no!"

"So, y'all didn't have any kind of love thing going on there?"

"No."

"So, was she gonna pay you to go?"

"She was gonna pay me to go with her and get this girl. That's why I said I did not like her. That's why I said the b**** is crazy."

"That's pretty far-fetched."

"When I saw Gerald at the club, I was like, 'hey…'"

"Wait, you said you didn't know he was crazy too. Why do you think that?"

"He's crazy. Both of them are crazy. I met them at the club. I didn't meet them there. I kind of ran into them. I was going to the bathroom, and Mark was like, 'Your toes are pretty.' And I was like, 'Thank you,' and I kept going. And he kept looking at me, and he was like, 'You could be a model.' I was like, 'I know y'all from somewhere.' And then I saw Gerald peek his head out, and I was like, 'Aw, hell, no!' Then I was like, 'I know who these people are.' I got up and walked in the other direction. When they finally realized who I was, I said, 'Okay, gotta go. Bye-bye.' I then went downstairs. Gerald then said to me, 'I really need you because this is not right what Lauryn's doing.' I was like, 'Okay, listen. I'm drunk. Here's my number.' I gave my number to Mark and left."

"Okay, before you go there, can we go back a little bit because I lost my train of thought."

"Okay."

"When you went to court with her… You're a smart girl. If I came up to you and said, 'Hey, baby. I want you in the courtroom with me in downtown Dallas in district court next Monday at 2:00 p.m.,' you're gonna say, 'What for?' You're not gonna say, 'Okay, yes, ma'am.'"

"No, no. I wouldn't."

"So, how did she get you in court?"

"She called me the day before and said, 'I have to go to court.' I said, 'Okay, well, I have meetings, so, what I can do is this… I don't know, I just can't come.' And she said, 'This is what we'll do—would you just write a letter?'"

"You're doing fine. Go back. Don't skip that."

"Okay, well, the b**** thinks I'm dumb. That's the thing that pisses me off. She thinks I'm dumb. That's why I was like, 'I can't deal with you.' Because she said I was gonna be pregnant at twenty-five. Don't wish it on me. Just because you're pregnant at thirty… Don't wish it on me. Okay? Because you're not married, you're pregnant, the man's acting stupid, don't wish nothing on me. Anyways, she said, 'Why don't you just write certain things down, and I'll write your paper for you.' Excuse me, I took three years of college, and I'm still in school. I believe I can do it myself."

"I'm not making you miss class tonight, am I?"

"Oh, no, 'cause then I would have to leave here."

"Okay, that works. She said that she'd write the things down, and all you had to do was sign it?"

"The letter was saying that I couldn't make it, and she was gonna take it up there. And her attorney, or whatever, was saying, 'Well, she needs to be there.'"

"For what?"

"This was for him, so they could lower his bail. And she didn't want them to lower the bail."

"What did she tell you she wanted you to say in the courtroom? She had to tell you that you were to say this and this and this."

"She wanted me to say that I heard him on the phone saying, 'I'm gonna kill you…'"

"But didn't you tell her then you didn't hear him?"

"Yeah, I told her that. I told her that I just heard her speaking. And she was like, 'Well, this is what I'm gonna tell them, and I want you to say that he was saying this.' I was like, 'Well, how's that gonna sound?' Hey, I'm gonna be sworn in. I'm not gonna go to jail. I'm not gonna go to jail for nobody."

"But then she told you that she wanted you to tell that you heard Gerald on the telephone?"

"And I told the lady that I heard her saying to somebody on the phone, 'You're gonna kill me 'cause you put me in jail.' That's what I heard her saying. I didn't hear anybody else. I mean, you could turn up the phone or whatever, but this is what I heard."

"That's all you heard?"

"That's all. That's me walking into the office."

"And then she said, 'Come to court and tell all that.'"

"Yeah, because she wanted his bail to stay the same."

"Okay."

"So, now when I'm in court, I didn't do anything. I wasted my time from work. I just sat there. Then, afterward, I was on my cell phone talking to everybody, and their Mama saying, 'Don't worry. I'm gonna be there. Everything is going to be okay. Your food will be there. Just leave me alone. Don't call me on my phone no more unless you wanna pay for my minutes.' And that was that."

"Are you studying theater?"

"No, but they said I should. They say I'm very dramatic. No, I'm studying to be a computer programmer. They make a lot of money."

"Are you really? Well, good for you."

"See, the thing I really want to do is be a lawyer, a criminal justice lawyer. The reason I was there in the first place is because she wanted to make sure that I was there. She [Lauryn]called me that night and I was talking to the officer because at the time my mom was staying with me. She called me that night, and she was making sure that I had my clothes right and looked professional. Look, I know how to dress. Don't dress me. 'How is your hair? I think I should come too and do your makeup so you can look all innocent'—and you know, I believe that I know how to do all these things. I did go to college for three years."

"All innocent—she wanted you to look all innocent."

"Yeah, like a good girl. Not one with an education or nothing like that, just a little nice and innocent girl with pigtails that she could put in my hair. She called me and said, 'I'll come and pick you up.' She came and picked me up early that morning and had gone to the place because she wanted to make sure that we were together so that I would be on time, and that was smart because I don't do time very well. I am late for everything.

"Okay, so after that then I said I met Gerald at the club and then Gerald called me and was like, 'Look, we need to talk about this.' I said okay. I met him on a Friday. We talked about it. We didn't really know what we were talking about at the trial. I said, 'Listen, I just want to drink, and it's on you. I just want to drink, and I'm gonna go home.' Gerald was like, 'Well, she's crazy. Her dad did this to her, and she was going through this whole…' I interrupted Gerald and said, 'I couldn't care less. I don't know what's going on between the two of you, but hey. Right now, we are here at a bar chilling, and I don't want to have any pictures snapped of me by this psycho.' I left the bar and met my date. Later that night, Gerald called me. I did not answer, and I called Gerald back and left a message on his answering machine. This is where my drama starts. I knew that Lauryn had his codes to his phones and computer, but I left a message anyway."

"He changed the code?"

"No, he did not change the code. Okay, so I had left him a message on his answering machine. Early that next morning, on a Saturday, Lauryn called me at my aunt's house. Lauryn kept calling back until I finally answered the phone. Lauryn said, 'You calling Gerald looks bad on the case.' I hung up the phone on her. That Sunday, I went to the club, and Mark and Gerald were there as always. Mark told me that Lauryn was over at Gerald's house, and he had told her everything. I was like, 'I couldn't care less. I don't want Gerald or Lauryn calling me ever again.' I even had my number changed at work so that it is private."

"Yeah, I could not find your work number the other day."

"They completely took my work number out of the Texas Technology system because of this. No one can find it. Then someone called my private number at work and said, 'You are getting careless.' I was like, 'Hello.' The voice said again, 'You're getting careless.' I was like again, 'Who is this?' The voice said, 'Your worst nightmare.' I know that that voice was Lauryn!"

"Was the voice male or female?"

"Female."

"Black, White, or Hispanic?"

"You can tell if it's a Black girl, you know. She got off the phone, and I was laughing and like, 'This girl is crazy.' Then she called again and hung up. I called my boss and told him about the calls."

"It was what?"

"It was like someone threatening me."

"I want to ask you a question and for you to think of a real serious answer to this one."

"Okay."

"She tried to get you to drive a getaway car to shoot somebody. Doesn't that cause you to believe that this woman could be seriously dangerous?"

"Yes."

"Aren't you at least moderately…? Aren't you a little concerned?"

"Yeah."

"And you haven't expressed that to the people at Texas Technology, that you're in fear of your life and at the very least in a hostile work environment?"

"Yeah. I told them, and they kind of took notice and took care of it a little bit, and it was, like, since it happened outside… They took care of it at work, and it's fine now. But if I'm at home…"

"But she is still there?"

"At Texas Technology?"

"Yeah."

"I think so. I'm not sure. I think they moved her to the third floor. I'm on the fifth, so I think they moved her to the third floor. When I just met her, my mother had just moved."

"I hope you don't let her know your mother just moved."

"I didn't let anybody know anything."

"How much was Lauryn going to pay you to drive the getaway car?"

"I don't remember."

"You can't remember?"

"Probably about five-something…"

"Five hundred dollars?"

"Yeah. I'm not even sure."

"Plus, all your expenses or something? Did y'all talk about it? Did y'all plan it or plot it?"

"Nah, she just kept talking about it."

"Talked about it five times, two times, three times…a number of times?"

"Probably a number of times. I told her, 'Why would you get her when you have Gerald? Get Gerald. God, not the girl. She just came down here for the funeral.' Just shoot her. She didn't want to kill her? She just wanted to shoot her? How dumb is that? If you are gonna do it, you might as well kill him, leave no evidence, put him in the car, get acid, put it on the body, and then no one ever knows. Come on, be smart. If you're gonna plot something, why just shoot the child? She shot this other girl, her friend, and she shot her in the leg, and I think she had to have it amputated."

"And she thought that was cool? Apparently, that's what she thought. She wanted to go do it is what you're telling me."

"Yeah, but is that cute? I said, 'Mama, the girl is crazy.' She was like, when all this stuff was happening, Lauryn was like, 'Patricia, you need to come home. You need to come to my house.' I was like, 'I'm not about to come to your house.' So, I stayed at my momma's house a few nights. My mom was scared really bad. I didn't get that much sleep while all this was going on."

"But you stayed home. You weren't getting sleep. You stayed home in fear."

"She didn't know exactly where I stayed, but she would, like, pop over and come get me."

"Get you how? Come give you flowers and candy?"

"No! Beat me up. Shoot me. Kill me. Something. I told my momma, 'Look, I'm about to purchase me a weapon 'cause if this child comes over to my house, I will shoot her and pull her into my house, and I am serious.' If she came into my house, I was going to try and take her out. From point-blank, I was gonna kill her. That's for real. Oh, yeah, I'm gonna retaliate, but I'm gonna do it legally. I'd rather put you in jail than beat you up than have to go to jail over something stupid."

"So, Patricia, are you retaliating now by changing your story, or are you telling the truth?"

"No, I am telling the truth. I would have told you this a long time ago if you had called me earlier. I mean, this is just the truth. She left messages on my answering machine and everything that I sent—all my work, all my paperwork—is signed, notarized, everything to them, and I have signed a paper."

"Who?"

"Texas Technology security. And somebody recently left a message on my work phone. This is after my work number had changed. Someone had called and said, 'I'm getting close to you, 9829 Walnut.' Only Lauryn and a few friends and family members knew that I stayed at 9829 Walnut, where she came and picked me up before. A couple of weeks later, after I stopped talking to Lauryn, somebody called my work line and left a message that said, 'You need to stop messing with my husband,' and she kept saying his name."

Patricia had provided the information that my attorneys needed in the deposition. Lauryn was attempting to use Patricia as an accomplice in an attempted murder of my ex-girlfriend. She had offered to pay money for Patricia to lie on her behalf. Lauryn was unscrupulous and willing to go to any extreme to destroy me.

Never Give Up!

Patricia's deposition provided us with the ammunition that we desperately needed. We knew that the evidence was on our side. She had revealed information that I had not known about Lauryn. Had she shot other people? Had she planned to shoot my ex-girlfriend? Had she offered to pay Patricia to testify against me? I felt a sense of relief, but I still had two charges hanging over my head, one of which was a felony.

It has often been said that the wheels of justice move slowly. It seemed that they were stuck in quicksand in my case. I had a great attorney and I had the truth on my side, yet I was still in serious legal trouble.

Over the next several weeks, I would frequently receive random calls from numbers that had been blocked so that I could not see the name or location of the person calling. One caller left this ominous message, "Gerald, we are watching you, you dirty bast***. You had better watch your back."

I was terrified! I knew that Lauryn was behind the calls. She knew that I traveled a lot for my job. I was afraid to sleep in hotels for fear that she would find a way to enter my room without my knowledge. She had broken into my apartment twice. I knew that she would do anything to keep me living in fear.

The fear, hypervigilance, and post-traumatic stress disorder were taking a toll on me emotionally. The smallest thing would cause me to jump. I was consumed with wondering what she would do to me next.

The therapy was helping, but I felt a deep sense of anxiety. I had experienced a lot of trauma during my childhood, but I had never had these symptoms. The worse the symptoms got, the more I began to drink. I knew that the self-medicating was getting the best of me.

On top of all my other challenges, I was pulled over by the police and was arrested for driving while intoxicated (DWI). My drinking was beginning to affect my personal and work life.

After the DWI, I continued to see my therapist. He provided me with a lot of support and guidance during this turbulent period. A few weeks later, I was arrested for a second DWI. Things were going from bad to worse. It seemed as if the walls were caving in around me.

I had abstained from drinking alcohol during my teenage and young adult years, but I began to drink heavily after I met Lauryn.

I had never heard of borderline personality disorder (BPD) until I had a conversation with Steve, my counselor. Steve was quite eccentric. He was a great counselor, but our sessions often ranged from politics to climate change. We both had deep intellectual curiosity, but I needed an effective counselor, not a thought partner. I was in a major life crisis and needed a real professional who could help me to process all that I had been through.

In a few short weeks, I was grieving the loss of my mother, managing major legal problems, about to become a father, and dealing with a woman with BPD. Steve had not diagnosed Lauryn; that would come later by a psychiatrist. Yet he suggested that her behaviors fit the pattern of BPD.

During one of our counseling sessions, Steve suggested that I read a book called *Stop Walking on Eggshells*. I purchased the CD and the book. I was amazed that Lauryn exhibited most of the signs and symptoms outlined in the book. Steve said that it would help me to better understand what I was dealing with. It gave me a window into her soul. I began to read the DSM-IV and later the DSM-V. They gave me keen insights into Lauryn's personality.

Some of the symptoms of BPD include chronic feelings of emptiness, impulsivity, identity disturbance, suicidal behavior, irritability, self-mutilating behavior, depression, anxiety, rage, and despair. As I read the book, it explained a lot about Lauryn.

Lauryn's childhood exhibited many of the similar patterns of other persons diagnosed with BPD: sexual abuse, abandonment, toxic stress, and lack of parental supervision and structure. Lauryn's family also had a long history of mental illness.

I asked my attorney if we could get a psychiatric evaluation done on Lauryn. He told me that we had to focus all our energy on winning the two cases that I was facing. Lauryn had recently filed a restraining order against me. I could not believe how easy it was to get a restraining order. I was not a threat to her. I had never exhibited violence against anyone in my entire life. Lauryn manipulated the assistant district attorney and the presiding judge to make me out to be a threat.

Protective orders and restraining orders are a great tool when used appropriately, but they are often used inappropriately, especially in child custody proceedings. Lauryn used them to punish me. I was never a threat to her or Sophia.

Within the next few months, I would be facing even more complex legal challenges. The restraining orders posed an even greater challenge. Lauryn was executing her strategy better than a corporate CEO. She also had masterful manipulation skills.

One Sunday evening, I was at my office doing paperwork when Lauryn called. I answered the phone.

Lauryn said, "Gerald, I am having problems with the pregnancy, and I need your help."

"Call 911," I responded.

A few minutes later, Lauryn was in front of my office door, beating on the window.

I met her at the door and spoke to her briefly.

"Please let me in. I need your help, Gerald," Lauryn pleaded.

I told her once again, "Please call 911, or I will call them for you."

I refused to let her enter into my office. She went and sat in her car, rubbing her stomach. After watching her rubbing her stomach for several minutes, I was afraid of what she would do next. A few hours later, I received a call that Lauryn was at the hospital. She alleged that I had hit her in the stomach while she was sitting in the car in front of my office.

Lauryn had struck herself in the stomach several times and blamed it on me! I quickly left the office and called my sister Belinda. Belinda had more wisdom than any person I knew. She was the matriarch of our family now that Muh had passed away. I had told her about everything I had gone through with Lauryn. She told me to call Detective Alex, the detective who was working on the prior cases. I had spoken with him several times regarding the previous cases. He knew that I was being truthful in my statements. I knew that he would listen. I called him up that evening and left a voice mail message. I spoke with him the next day. He told me that he had been assigned to the case.

Detective Alex asked me several probing questions. He asked if I was okay with an interview. I told him, "Yes." After several minutes of questioning, the detective told me that he believed my story. My hands were too large to have made the marks on her stomach that she had alleged. She had also stated that I punched her in the stomach while she was sitting in the car. The trajectory of the punches to her stomach from outside of the car would have made that impossible.

I was not arrested on this charge while it was being investigated. The charge was later dismissed, but I was shaken to the core. I knew that she would go to any means to put me away. She wanted me out of the way. She wanted me in prison. Whenever she didn't get what she wanted when she wanted it, she would try and remove the person obstructing her.

I also feared for the baby. Lauryn was hitting herself in the stomach, bleeding profusely while several months pregnant. Would the baby be safe? Would the baby survive?

After the assault charges were dismissed, I did not hear from Lauryn for a few weeks. I finally had some peace. I continued to see my counselor on a weekly basis. That helped me to cope to some degree. I was still having signs of PTSD, anxiety, and depression. The drinking only made my depression worse. My counselor encouraged me to stop drinking, but I couldn't at the time. I was dealing with too many pressing problems.

After the deposition and hearing in February and March, my attorney suggested that I cooperate with Lauryn. The plan was to get as much information as possible that could help my case. I would need to act as if I were interested in a relationship with Lauryn. I was disgusted with the thought of being with her. After much skepticism, I agreed to cooperate. Early on the morning of April 22, Lauryn pounded on my door. I allowed her to come into my apartment, the same apartment where she had assaulted me months earlier.

Lauryn said that she had been in a local hospital. I asked her if she needed to see a doctor, and she said, "No." She stayed at my apartment for a few hours and then left. Later that evening, Lauryn reappeared at my apartment. She told me that I did not care that she had been sick. She threatened to spray me with mace if I moved. She then blocked the front door. She had a wild look in her eyes as she talked loudly and held the can of mace spray toward me. While swinging her arms, Lauryn broke several items in my apartment. I sat and listened to Lauryn's tirades from eight o'clock that evening until five o'clock the next morning. Lauryn had badly bruised my right leg and right lower arm with a cup and wooden elephant that she had thrown at me.

After all the harm that Lauryn had caused, she wanted to attend church with me that morning. Lauryn was raised a Jehovah's Witness. I made up an excuse why I could not attend church with her. I told Lauryn that she had held me hostage for several hours and that she must get some help. I chose not to call the police out of fear that the tables would be turned against me. I didn't know how much longer I could go along with this plan. It was too painful and dangerous.

Lauryn constantly threatened me about going to the judges or assistant district attorneys if I did not cooperate with her. She eventually left my apartment on Sunday afternoon. It was the break that I so desperately needed.

A few days later, Lauryn called and stated that she wanted to meet once again at my apartment. I refused. After the last encounter, I packed my bags and planned to visit my sisters in East Texas. As soon as I exited my apartment, Lauryn pulled up beside my car and turned her vehicle sideways, blocking my ability to move forward.

Somehow, I was able to navigate my way around her vehicle and escape.

After I escaped, she continued to follow and call me while making threats against me. She attempted to run me off the highway on two separate occasions. She loved to run vehicles off the highway. I decided to exit the highway in an attempt to hide from Lauryn. I stopped at a Chevron station and ran into the store. I spoke to the attendant and asked for him to call the police. I then told him not to do so out of fear of retaliation.

After Lauryn threatened me in the Chevron parking lot, I ran into a residential area, leaving my car parked at Chevron. I hitchhiked a ride to the Fair Park area of Dallas.

After that episode, I told my attorney that I could not follow through on the plan any longer. I was fearful I would be killed. Lauryn was getting more unstable by the day. She was also getting more violent.

A few days later, Lauryn called and apologized for pressing charges against me. I recorded her statement:

> I apologize for pressing charges against you, Gerald. I made up the charges, and I am sorry. My girlfriends encouraged me to make up a story. It was not my idea. The assistant district attorneys told me what to say. I will find a way out, but I do not want to get myself into trouble by saying that I lied. Please accept my apology.

I knew that Lauryn was not serious when she left the message. I did not accept her apology. Her apologies were always on her terms. She would apologize one moment and then strike at me the next. At least Lauryn had confessed to what she had done.

In so many ways, my life seemed to be falling apart. I was in legal and financial trouble. I had a daughter on the way unexpectedly. I was constantly being threatened and harassed. Lauryn knew that she had me in her clutches.

In the summer of 2000, I met the woman I would ultimately marry. Her name was Crystal. She embodied everything that I wanted and needed in a relationship. Crystal had been recently divorced. We both had gone through painful situations in our lives. We were both there for one another. It was a new beginning during a difficult time.

Crystal had two daughters, Moriah and Megan. They were great additions to my life as well. Crystal was everything that Lauryn was not. She was caring, patient, compassionate, and kind. I felt that God had answered my prayers.

On July 24, 2000, I received an urgent call from Lauryn. She had called from a Dallas hospital. She asked me to come to the hospital so that I could see our daughter, Sophia. I felt a range of emotions. Was she my daughter? Was she healthy? What did she look like? I was afraid to visit her at the hospital. My attorneys and sisters had advised me not to visit her for fear of retaliation. I also had a restraining order against me. I didn't know if this was a setup or not. Lauryn pleaded with me to come and sign the birth certificate. I refused.

I felt different after I received that call. I did not have any biological children and hadn't planned on having children without being married. What would I do if she were my daughter? How could I have a relationship with her after everything that I had gone through? How could I work around these constraints?

A few weeks later, I received yet another call from Lauryn. I will never forget the words that she said to me in a hurried voice: "Gerald, I can't stop pulling her hair and spraying her in the face with water!"

Lauryn was spraying Sophia in the face with water and pulling her hair. She couldn't stop doing it. I thought that she would drown her in the bathtub!

Lauryn kept repeating those frantic words, "I can't stop." I asked her to please stop pulling her hair and spraying her with water in the face and to get some help. I feared that she would drown and kill Sophia. I called and reported the incident to CPS. CPS never conducted a formal investigation. Thankfully, Sophia survived.

After this incident, my sisters wanted to visit with Sophia. I gave them Lauryn's contact information. A few days later, Wilma, Maria, Wanita, and Belinda drove to Dallas and visited with Lauryn and Sophia. Sophia was only three weeks old at the time. They were excited to see her. Most importantly, they wanted to see if she resembled me. They took pictures of her and brought them to my apartment. It was evident that she was my daughter.

My sisters were the moral support that I needed at the time. We spent a few days together drinking coffee and talking about Muh. She had died only a few months earlier. I didn't have a chance to grieve. I was grateful to have sisters who loved and supported me. They, too, were fearful for my life. They knew that Lauryn was a danger to Sophia and me.

After my sisters' visit, I didn't hear from Lauryn for a few weeks. I was waiting for the next shoe to drop. I knew that we would be going to court soon to work out child support and visitation arrangements. Before we could go to family court, Lauryn had called and reported that I had violated the protective order by threatening to kill her and Sophia! She wanted to make sure that I would never have any unsupervised contact with my own daughter. She made me out to be the monster. In her mind, she was the angel, and I was the demon.

A few days later, a hearing was held on the protective order. Lauryn appeared in court with her attorney. I stood alongside my attorney and approached the bench. Both attorneys made their arguments before the judge. The presiding judge asked me about my height and weight. I did not understand why this had anything to do with the protective order. Lauryn and her attorney had made the case that Lauryn was a small woman, and I was a tall Black man. So, I must have been the aggressor.

I responded to the judge, "Your Honor, I am six feet, seven inches, and two hundred pounds. I have not made any threats against Lauryn Burns."

My attorney put up a vigorous defense, but the judge had already made up his mind. The judge had assumed that because I was much larger—and darker—than Lauryn, I must have been the guilty party.

Within less than twelve months, Lauryn had filed several false charges against me: criminal trespassing, phone harassment, terroristic threat, simple assault, retaliation, assault, protective orders (for herself and Sophia), and violations of protective orders.

My strong support system and faith in God gave me strength. I had never faced such overwhelming challenges before. I still had a lot of people who believed in me. The only thing that separated me from the other Black men in the criminal justice system was that I had the resources and relationships to fight back.

I was speaking with two different detectives at the Dallas Police Department. They believed my story, but Lauryn was putting pressure on the district attorney's office and the courts to get me off the streets. I didn't realize at the time the power that prosecutors have in a case. Lauryn had formed a bond with the female prosecutors in Dallas County. They supported her every move. They told her what to say and what moves to make.

It didn't hurt that Bob Hill, the Dallas district attorney at the time, was extremely tough as a prosecutor. My attorney knew him and set up a meeting with the head of the felony division at the DA's office. The message was always, "Let the system work. If he did not commit a crime, the system will not convict him." I was living proof that this adage does not always apply. At least, it wasn't operative in my case. The criminal justice system wasn't working impartially.

That story sounded great, but the justice system had never worked the same for Blacks and Whites in Dallas County, Texas. There was a long and sordid history of racial bias.

Rather than give in, I fought back every step of the way. I received great news by the end of December 2000. The assault, harassment, and retaliation charges were all dismissed. I only had to deal with the protective order, which was still in place. I knew that things would get worse now that Sophia was born. First, Lauryn was obsessed with money. She wanted to get the maximum amount of child support possible and to make sure that I didn't get visitation rights with Sophia. I was not concerned about the child support. I had already begun to give money to Lauryn to care for Sophia. Lauryn believed that I would stop fighting and give up my parental rights. She didn't know that I would never give up!

Things Fall Apart

A huge burden was lifted after all of the pending charges were dismissed. I knew that I had been innocent all along. Now that Sophia had been born, we were becoming involved with the Dallas County family court system. Lauryn knew that, if I had a criminal conviction, I would have no chance of getting regular unsupervised visits with Sophia, let alone custody. She also knew that a conviction could affect my job and career.

After much deliberation and prayer, I began to informally meet with Lauryn at a local mall in an open space. I was careful to visit with her in public spaces so that my interactions with her would be on camera. I also had friends who were in the area so that they could respond if needed.

Sophia was a bundle of joy. I was glad to see her, but afraid of what Lauryn would do next. She talked a lot about us getting back together and raising Sophia. As badly as I wanted to be there for my daughter, I could not be in a relationship with Lauryn. That was out of the question. I knew that she was having a hard time adjusting to motherhood. I didn't know if she suffered from postpartum depression.

In early 2001, Lauryn and I had our first family court hearing. A paternity test was ordered. Sophia was my biological daughter. Lauryn was angry that a paternity test had been ordered in the first place. The judge also ordered that I make payments to Lauryn for the care of Sophia until formal arrangements could be set by the court. I had already been giving money to Lauryn to support Sophia for months. I kept a detailed record of payments that I made to Lauryn.

After the court hearing, I gave Lauryn an $800 check as the judge had ordered. A couple of days later, I noticed that $1,600 had been withdrawn from my checking account, not $800. I looked into the situation further with my bank. The bank told me that a person with my checking account and routing number had withdrawn an additional $800 from my account. I told them that she did not have authorization to do so. This was theft. I spoke with several people at the bank and attempted to file charges, but the bank authorities were not open to charges being filed. Once again, Lauryn had victimized me, but I could not get the authorities to respond on my behalf.

Through my attorneys, I found that Lauryn had recently lost her job at Texas Technology. She was terminated in part due to the threats made against Patricia. She had also utilized Texas Technology equipment and lied about threats made against her while at her place of employment. Lauryn was now trying to get her teacher's certification to teach math. I knew that this was a dangerous path both for Lauryn and the students. Lauryn did not have the mental stability needed to teach children.

After one of our many hearings in family court, Lauryn informed the courts that I had once again threatened to kill Sophia and her. "He threatened to kill both of us," she said as tears streamed down her face. The judge looked upon her with great sympathy. The presiding judge ordered that I not have any contact with Lauryn or Sophia. Lauryn's strategy was working perfectly.

Lauryn was working on several fronts to destroy me. She was a technology expert. Lauryn hacked my e-mail at work and sent an e-mail to me and several others at my place of employment. She made it appear that I had sent this threatening e-mail to her:

> I don't give a f*** about you, Sophia or anybody else. Judge Nichols and Judge Collins can suck my fat d***. With regard to child support, I will find a way to lower those f****** payments. You chose to have Sophia against my will, so you will find a way to support her. Lauryn, I know that I have beat on you, but do you keep having to bring it up in court? I love you and I know that I said I would kill you and the baby but I

was angry. Now I got my attorney believing you would kill me. I know, I lied, but hey, the show must go on. I am going to destroy you and put you in jail and will file as many false charges as I can against you and I will try my best to make up as many lies on you so that the courts will take Sophia from you—believe me Lauryn, I'm good. I've been at this business for years.

This was one of many phantasmagoric statements that Lauryn had made up. It was puzzling that the courts and prosecutors would often take her statements as factual. Lauryn would often use sexually explicit language in her e-mails and affidavits. She had a constant fear and obsession with sex and sexual abuse. I do not know if this had anything to do with her childhood sexual abuse or mental illness, or both.

My employer decided not to file a suit against her for hacking our e-mail system. My job knew that I would never send such an e-mail. Lauryn used every trick in the book to build a case against me. Unfortunately, I had spent tens of thousands of dollars just to defend myself against her allegations.

During one of my counseling sessions, Steve suggested that we meet with the Dallas deputy police chief. He listened to my concerns. They could not understand how all this had happened without any material evidence against me.

The meeting with the Dallas Police Department deputy police chief was held on Tuesday, September 11, 2001, the day of the terrorist attacks in New York, Pennsylvania, and Washington! I witnessed the twin towers being attacked while I was trying to save my life from Lauryn's vicious attacks! I found it all ironic.

Early in the family court process, Lauryn appeared in family court with a new attorney. I could tell from the outset that this was not a typical attorney-client relationship. I knew that Lauryn was willing to use sex to get free legal representation. She would give sexual favors if it worked to her advantage. Lauryn's new attorney was Matthew Nimpson, a Black attorney with a boyish grin. He seemed elated to be representing Lauryn. It was evident that they had a romantic relationship.

During the hearing, Attorney Nimpson briefly spoke with my attorney. My attorney, Attorney Janet Martin, told me that there was something not right about him. He didn't work with her as attorneys had in the past. He was in Lauryn's clutches. He was not willing to meet with my attorney to discuss the case unless required to do so by the presiding judge. Attorney Nimpson had run a rather successful practice focusing on juvenile and criminal law. He didn't have experience in family law. I could tell that he would do anything to defend Lauryn.

After the second restraining order, I still attempted to get temporary visits with Sophia. Lauryn alleged that I might sexually abuse Sophia. I thought that this would not be taken seriously by the court. I had worked with children all my adult life. I had been a youth minister, mentor, home hospice volunteer, chaplain, and worked for a nonprofit that worked with troubled young people. I babysat during my college years. It was devastating to hear the allegation. I was not surprised. My sister had told me many years ago that Lauryn would stoop to any level, including alleging sexual abuse.

After the allegation was made, my attorney suggested that I take an Abel Assessment conducted by a licensed professional. The Abel Assessment is utilized to determine whether adults have sexual interests in minors. I was devastated to have to take such a test, yet I went along with it so that I could have unsupervised visits with my daughter. Until the Abel Assessment was completed, I was ordered to have court-ordered, supervised visits with Sophia. I paid $90 an hour to visit with my daughter once a week while a clinician observed my every move. I followed through on this temporary arrangement for months until the evaluation was completed.

The supervised visits were devastating. I could not believe that the judge had made such an order based on such frivolous allegations. There was no credible basis for supervised visits. I was paying $90 per hour to visit with my daughter while Lauryn was causing emotional and physical harm to Sophia. Lauryn was the one who had almost drowned Sophia.

My Abel Assessment tests came back as normal. My attorney presented this information to the court. I also took a lie detector test to prove that I had not threatened Lauryn or my daughter. The lie detector test came back normal as well. I thought that it would be smooth sailing after the test results came back in my favor.

During one of my last supervised visits, I watched as Lauryn pulled up to pick up Sophia. While picking up Sophia, Lauryn became irritated for some unknown reason. She quickly pulled in front of a BMW and blocked him in so that his car could not move forward. Lauryn quickly got out of her vehicle and beat on his window, yelling cuss words. The gentleman in the car refused to lower his windows. The woman who sat on the passenger side was clearly in fear as Lauryn beat on his window. After a few minutes spent throwing a temper tantrum, Lauryn got into her vehicle, picked up Sophia, and strapped her in the car seat. I walked up to the guy driving the car. He and his girlfriend were visibly shaken.

I gave him my business card and told him about my legal situation. He was a prominent attorney in Dallas. We exchanged business cards and promised to call one another. I contacted him several times, but he refused to return my call.

He would become one of several victims of Lauryn's road rage. While she was pregnant, she had two automobile accidents. One of the accidents was serious and badly injured her father. Once again, Lauryn got away without any consequences. People were downright afraid of Lauryn. Far too often, the victims were afraid to come forward for fear of Lauryn retaliating against them. This strategy always seemed to work to her advantage. Lauryn knew how to strike fear in others.

After the Abel Assessment, my attorney worked diligently to get me unsupervised visits with Sophia. The judge issued temporary orders for me to have unsupervised visits. I was pleased that the judge had issued these temporary orders, even though the restraining orders remained in place. I found that protective orders and false allegations are often used in child custody cases. The person that makes the allegations first is most likely to have an upper hand. Lauryn always struck first!

Lauryn now had the weapon that she needed. She had an attorney and lover who would do anything legal or illegal to help her. It appeared that he was afraid of her. Lauryn liked to get information on her lovers that she could use against them to exploit or bribe them.

During one of our exchanges with Sophia, Attorney Nimpson showed up with Lauryn at 9:00 p.m. on a Sunday evening.

I found out through one of Lauryn's friends that Lauryn and Attorney Nimpson were dating. He was married but was still constantly with Lauryn. Lauryn did not have any boundaries. She showed up to watch his kids play sports while his wife was present. She even showed up at the church that he attended and sat in the same row with him and his family during the entire church service. Lauryn would go to any length to make per point.

Attorney Nimpson's wife was afraid of Lauryn. Lauryn had made several threats against her. Rather than protect his wife, Attorney Nimpson attended to Lauryn's every need. I began to wonder if she was blackmailing him. I would later find out that Lauryn had threatened to have his law license terminated if he did not do as she wanted.

The unsupervised visits with Sophia were joyful. I spent several weekends with her. I had to deal with constant interference by Lauryn, but I was at least getting to see my daughter. I began to wonder if Lauryn had caused some severe emotional damage to Sophia. Every time I returned Sophia to her mother, she would scream and pull on me. "Dad, please don't take me back to mommy," she cried. It was devastating to see her not want to go home. I was determined more than ever to save Sophia from Lauryn.

Determination

I was determined not to allow Lauryn to stop me from seeing Sophia. She kept putting up roadblocks. I knew that Lauryn was severely mentally ill and unstable. Sophia was being hurt in the process. Yet there was no documentation to validate or verify her illness. I spoke with my attorney and asked that she request a psychiatric examination.

Lauryn had always fought any mental examination. I asked my attorney to speak with Matthew Nimpson to see if both of us could be ordered to have a psychiatric evaluation. I agreed to pay the fees for both examinations. Judge Gaston initially appeared reticent to order mental examinations. She was known to work to keep children with their biological parents whenever possible. After awarding me unsupervised visitation, the judge began to determine custody of Sophia. We both agreed for Judge Gaston to hear the case.

After a few weeks of deliberation, Judge Gaston finally ordered that a mental examination be conducted on both Lauryn and me. I was excited. In addition, a social study had been ordered. I hoped that the social workers, psychiatrist, and judge would finally see that Lauryn was severely mentally ill and not capable of caring adequately for Sophia.

A few weeks later, the home study was assigned to a social worker, Kirsten Bradley. Kirsten appeared very professional. I met with her a few days later in her office. Our interview lasted for several hours. I could tell that she was overwhelmed with all that had occurred. She appeared to be a neutral arbiter. I was always concerned that Lauryn or her attorney had done something unethical to get the outcome that they wanted.

I told Kirsten about my drinking. She was concerned that I had been arrested for two DWIs. I shared with her my entire life story from childhood to the present. I could tell that she was concerned about my drinking and travel schedule. I had developed a parenting plan that I thought would work well to support Sophia. My sisters were going to help me raise her. Crystal and I had also grown closer. Megan and Moriah were close to Sophia's age.

Kirsten asked a lot of questions about the need for the Abel Assessment. I shared with her my anxiety and "situational" depression. I had never had any of these symptoms prior to meeting Lauryn. I had been a social drinker but had never drank heavily. I shared with her my concerns about Sophia's safety with Lauryn. I told her about the incident when Lauryn sprayed Sophia in the face with water and pulled her hair uncontrollably. I was concerned that Sophia's mistreatment had affected her development.

The few times that I had kept Sophia, I noticed that she would stare into space for very long periods of time. She would also have very intense nightmares, often jumping out of bed. When I would have my visitations, Sophia never wanted me to take her back to her mother. I also noticed that Sophia was not very talkative. She would go for hours without saying anything. I had worked with young people for many years. She did not appear to be meeting many of her developmental milestones. I also knew that emotional and physical abuse could have a negative impact on a child's development.

During our next court hearing, Kirsten presented a preliminary report to the court. She shared her concerns about my drinking and travel schedule. She also shared with the court her several concerns about Lauryn: that Lauryn had threatened and even pushed her as she left Lauryn's apartment! Kirsten didn't feel safe around Lauryn. She expressed to the court concerns about her own personal safety. Kirsten had been too intrusive for Lauryn. She expressed concerns about Lauryn being fired from her job as an engineer and about her prior criminal history as well. Near the end of her report, Kirsten stated:

> The first concern is that the mother appears to be enmeshed with Sophia. The mother also identified on more than one occasion that Sophia

is her best friend. This behavior by the mother appears to demonstrate a relationship which will hinder Sophia's ability to develop independently through her appropriate developmental stages. The mother is engaging in these activities for self-serving reasons rather than the child's best interest, as evidenced by her need to process her own emotions and feelings regarding adult issues with Sophia. These adult conversations will quickly become confusing and overwhelming to a child of such a young age. The mother reported that she is reading the dictionary and reading and teaching Sophia material that is advanced. The mother's exposure of Sophia to developmentally advanced materials could lead Sophia to extreme frustration at an early age because content mastery of advanced material is not possible for a child within Sophia's developmental stage.

The mother also appears to have unrealistic perceptions of Sophia's medical needs. The mother's alleged inaccurate perceptions of Sophia's medical needs has led to the mother reporting that she will lie awake at night and watch her daughter sleep and administer medications. These types of behaviors by the mother cause question as to the possibility of a projected fictitious disorder.

I was concerned about her statement that Lauryn may have a "projected fictitious disorder." Near the end of the report, Kirsten suggested temporary foster care as an option. I was taken aback by that option. I had spent my entire adult career fighting for children. I had spent a lot of time and resources seeking to care for my own daughter. I felt that Kirsten had not taken the false allegations against me seriously. I had developed a parenting plan that would have been good for Sophia.

Judge Gaston didn't like the notion of foster care as an option. I was grateful. Even though I was single and traveled a lot, I knew that I could have provided great care for Sophia. I had a strong network of family members that supported me. I also had the finances to provide daycare and other forms of support. My child support was set at nearly $1,400 per month, not including health insurance. Sophia was my only child.

I didn't make a strong argument about the child support. I just wanted to have an opportunity to have a normal relationship with my daughter.

A well-respected psychiatrist finally conducted the evaluations on both Lauryn and me. Dr. Anton met separately with Lauryn and conducted the psychiatric evaluations. The psychiatrist conducted a verbal and written assessment/evaluation. A few weeks later, my attorney shared with me the psychiatric evaluation. My evaluation stated that I was dealing with "situational depression," anxiety, and post-traumatic stress disorder. Lauryn's psychiatric evaluation stated that she had characteristics of "borderline personality disorder, schizoaffective disorder, and narcissistic personality disorder."

After reading the evaluations, I met with my counselor to try to get a professional opinion on what this diagnosis meant. My counselor said in no uncertain terms, "This means that you are in danger and your daughter is in danger." Everything that I had read in *Stop Walking on Eggshells* was true. People with this disorder have difficulty maintaining relationships. Some of them are violent and confrontational and constantly in conflict. I read up on schizoaffective disorder. Many of the symptoms mentioned were remarkably similar to my experience with Lauryn. She was delusional and often had marked changes in her mood.

I immediately thought back to my visit with Lauryn's mother a few years back. Lauryn had shared with me that her mom suffered from paranoid schizophrenia and her dad suffered from bipolar disorder. I began to wonder if there was some genetic link with Lauryn. I began to read several books to better understand schizoaffective disorder. Lauryn would often have delusions and hallucinations. I experienced this firsthand while she lived with me for a few days. Lauryn's family members had also told me about her frequent hallucinations.

Lauryn was also extremely controlling, deceptive, and retaliatory. She could also be violent. I began to wonder if Lauryn was self-aware of her behaviors and could control them. I wondered if the courts would finally take notice and stop believing her extreme antics. I hoped that I could use this report to help convince the court to award me custody so that Sophia could have a normal life. Everybody knew that Lauryn had very severe mental problems, but I finally had proof.

During our next court hearing, Judge Gaston read the psychiatric evaluations. Kirsten was present. After a thorough review, Judge Gaston ordered that Lauryn and I attend a mediation with a well-respected African American psychologist, Dr. Treat. She ran a private practice and taught at a local university. A few days later, Lauryn and I met with Dr. Treat.

"What do you all see as your major challenges?" Dr. Treat asked.

"I don't have any challenges. Gerald is trying to take my daughter away from me. That is the problem," Lauryn stated.

"Gerald?" Dr. Treat asked.

"I think that our biggest challenge is that Lauryn keeps presenting obstacles in court. I simply want to have a relationship with my daughter and get to see her as often as possible."

"Thanks, Gerald," Dr. Treat said, breathing heavily. "How can I help both of you?"

"You can't f****** help us. Gerald is the problem. He thinks that he can use his title and position to get his way. I bet that he knows you."

"No, we do not know one another, Lauryn," Dr. Treat stated.

The first meeting was off to a bad start. The court ordered that I pay for the mediation costs. I was already struggling financially. I was paying extremely high child support, health insurance, two attorneys, and now mediation costs. I had paid $90 an hour to visit with Sophia during supervised visits. Now I was paying for a mediation that was going nowhere.

Lauryn had cussed at Dr. Treat several times during our visits. She would meet with us one-on-one and then as a couple. Dr. Treat was trying to get some form of agreement for the court. I was cooperating with her. Lauryn refused to cooperate. After our fifth visit, Dr. Treat shared that she would prepare a report for the court. She shared with us the risk of having Sophia removed from both of us if we did not cooperate. I could tell that she was exasperated.

I knew that the mediation would not work. Lauryn never was able to negotiate anything. It was her way or the highway. She never thought about what was best for Sophia. During our next hearing with Judge Gaston, she read the report from Dr. Treat. I could tell from her demeanor that she was exasperated. I was following through on everything that Judge Gaston had ordered. Dr. Treat would no longer continue with the mediation.

Judge Gaston asked both attorneys to work out a plan that both Lauryn and I could agree to. I felt at the time that Lauryn was not going to be held accountable by the court. Lauryn very seldomly followed through on the court's orders. Somehow, she always seemed to get away with it.

Lauryn knew that after the psychiatric evaluations, threats to Kirsten, and conflict with Dr. Treat, she was in danger of losing custody of Sophia. Lauryn had been on the run all her adult life. Once she had destroyed relationships or had legal problems, she would move to another city or state and create even more victims. Lauryn knew that her lies were catching up with her. Matthew Nimpson knew it too.

Easter

During the spring of 2003, things were getting better for the moment. I was having frequent unsupervised visits with Sophia. Judge Gaston had allowed Sophia to spend a few weeks with me. The courts were looking more favorably at me as the custodial parent. We were in the throes of a custody dispute. While the mediation with Dr. Treat had not worked out, Judge Gaston was beginning to see signs of Lauryn's mental illness. She had received reports from a psychiatrist, a psychologist, and the home study social worker. They had all raised concerns about Lauryn's mental instability.

I was excited to pick up Sophia on the Easter weekend of April 20, 2003. Easter Sundays were typically joyous occasions for us. I sometimes preached on Easter Sunday, but not this year. Crystal and I had Sophia with us on Easter weekend. We attended a local church in Fort Worth. After the Easter service, we went to eat lunch together as a family.

After dinner, Crystal went with me to return Sophia to Lauryn after a delightful weekend. Crystal typically didn't go with me to drop off Sophia. I had learned with Lauryn to always expect the unexpected. The evening before, we had bought Sophia a colorful purple dress and white shoes. She looked angelic. All of this was new to her. We wanted to give her an opportunity to experience what it was like to be in a stable, loving family.

After church, we went to eat dinner and take pictures in the bluebonnets. Sitting in the bluebonnets in a purple dress, Sophia was beautiful. She seemed to enjoy the uninterrupted joy of just being a child. No pressures. No worries. No fears. No beatings. No threats. No manipulation. No drama. Before we knew it, it was time to take Sophia back to Lauryn. Crystal was driving while Sophia sat in the back seat. We drove to Valley View Mall so that we could conduct our exchange.

I always felt somewhat uneasy when we were about to do our exchanges. Sophia never wanted to leave us and go back with her mother. As soon as we entered the mall entrance, I could see Lauryn's light-green Ford Explorer from a distance. She was facing the mall entrance. I slowly pulled up parallel to her SUV.

Lauryn quickly walked to the passenger's side of Crystal's vehicle. She was walking fast toward us while talking on her cell phone. I began to help get Sophia out of her car seat.

As I was unbuckling the three-point harness on Sophia's car seat, Lauryn yelled to Crystal, "Did you tell my baby to shut the f*** up? Did you, b****?"

Crystal said, "No, I didn't… I wouldn't talk to a child like that."

Lauryn screamed, "Then I guess that Sophia is lying… So, you are calling my baby a liar?"

At that moment, Lauryn began to try to kick Crystal in the head. I did my best to get control of the situation. Sophia was in the back seat crying profusely.

I was finally able to get Sophia out of the car. I gave Sophia to Lauryn and then we quickly sped out of the parking lot. We both left the mall in a panic. Where did this come from? Why was she attempting to hit Crystal? Why was she so explosive? Crystal had been really good to Sophia. She had cared for her as she did her own daughters.

After we calmed down, we began to think about what all this meant. Lauryn hardly did anything without a motive. She always planned things out. There were times that she was impulsive, but she always seemed to have an ulterior motive.

Lauryn remained in the mall parking lot crying profusely and plotting her next move. She filed a police report with the Dallas Police Department alleging that Crystal had attempted to run over both Sophia and her with her vehicle. The charges filed were two counts of attempted vehicular homicide against a minor and adult. Crystal would face over thirty years in prison if convicted! I had been

Lauryn's target for years. I had grown to live with threats from her. Now she was targeting Crystal.

Lauryn had a history of targeting the girlfriend or wife to get them out of the way so that she could have the man that she desired. Get rid of the woman and you can have the man. I had heard a sermon earlier that morning about resurrection possibilities. I once again felt a deep sense of agony for what I knew lay ahead for Crystal and me.

A few days later, Detective Elk with the Dallas Police Department shared with Crystal the charges that had been made against her. Lauryn had reported the following about the incident:

> Crystal took off in the vehicle at a high rate of speed around the parking lot at Valley View Mall. I became fearful and picked up my daughter. Crystal then drove the vehicle at a high rate of speed directly in the path of my daughter and me, attempting to strike us with her vehicle. I dialed 911 on my cell phone. When Crystal had stopped the vehicle, I then stopped to pick up Sophia. I believe that if I did not run away from the path of the vehicle, my daughter and I would have been struck. We received no injuries.

Detective Elk interviewed Crystal a few days after the incident occurred. Crystal's statement was as follows:

> Gerald and I were dropping Sophia off at Valley View Mall. We were running late and Gerald called Lauryn and let her know that we would be late arriving at the mall. When we arrived at the mall, Lauryn was parked facing the mall. I was driving and pulled up next to Lauryn's SUV. Lauryn got out of her vehicle and started to yell profanities toward me. Gerald was getting Sophia out of the back seat when Lauryn

came around the car to open the passenger door and tried to hit and kick me. Gerald had gotten Sophia out of the back seat and was trying to stop Lauryn from kicking and hitting me. Gerald had tried to separate Lauryn without her saying that he had assaulted her. I then got in the driver's seat and inched the car forward so that Gerald could get in the vehicle and we left the scene. I am willing to take a polygraph.

"What if I told you that I have a videotape of the incident?" Detective Elk said.

Crystal said, "Great. It will show that Lauryn was kicking at me through the passenger door of the car."

According to the offense report, Detective Elk asked Lauryn to come in so that she could interview her about the entire incident. Lauryn said that she spoke with her attorney and said that it was unusual for the person making the complaint to come in and talk with a detective. A few days later, Lauryn showed up with Attorney Nimpson. As always, Lauryn had prepared a written affidavit. Detective Elk asked her if the statements were true and correct.

Lauryn replied, "Yes."

The detective then produced a tape and questioned Lauryn about the offenses. Lauryn then asked for her affidavit back and stated that she wanted to recant what she had written.

Lauryn then began to cry and stated, "Crystal did not try and run my daughter over."

Detective Elk advised Lauryn that she needed to be truthful. She allowed Lauryn to leave the room to think about her statement. Attorney Nimpson came back in to speak with Detective Elk to advise her of what Lauryn had said. In the presence of her attorney, Lauryn wrote an affidavit stating that Crystal did not accelerate her car toward her or her daughter, Sophia. Lauryn and her attorney were informed that this and the related offenses were unfounded and that charges for making a false police report might be made.

Charges were never filed against Lauryn for filing the false police reports. She had filed over eight false police reports against me and now two against Crystal. The Dallas Police Department did not bring a charge against Lauryn for repeatedly filing false police reports. This only emboldened her.

After the false police report filed against Crystal, we were in disbelief. How could this be allowed to continue without consequences? How could she get away with this? How could her attorney help Lauryn continue to manufacture lies of epic proportions? Lauryn was masterful at getting out of impossible situations. Crystal and I were both victims. Yet, her greatest victim was Sophia. She didn't yet have a voice.

Crystal and I were both exasperated. No matter what Lauryn did, there appeared to be no legal consequences. At least, not yet.

The Darkest Hour

Crystal and I were both exhausted after Lauryn's efforts to have Crystal incarcerated on false charges. After this incident, Crystal and I separated. The separation was hard on both of us and Megan and Moriah. We both thought that it would be best for us to separate due to safety concerns.

It has been said that the darkest hour is just before dawn. After several months of hearings, a home study, false allegations, an Abel Assessment, psychiatric evaluations, and false police reports, I was getting weary. I knew that Lauryn would make another move. She would never stop until I was dead or just gave up.

Giving up for me was never an option. I had faced too many adversities in my childhood to give up now. I hadn't allowed racism and poverty to destroy me. I would not allow Lauryn to destroy me either. I knew that if I didn't get Sophia away from Lauryn, her future would be in jeopardy. Lauryn had almost killed Sophia by punching herself in the stomach while she was seven months pregnant. She had almost drowned Sophia at one month old. What could happen next?

The answer came a few weeks later. I had picked Sophia up for a weekend visitation. I allowed Sophia to stay with a close friend's wife, who was a social worker, for a few hours. Everything seemed to go well over the weekend. I dropped Sophia off with Lauryn Sunday evening as usual. A few hours later, I received a call from Lauryn.

Lauryn yelled, "Sophia has a burn on her finger, and she was abused by some boy while she was with the babysitter." Lauryn screamed, "Gerald, you allowed this to happen to our daughter!"

I knew that she was setting the stage for something larger.

I had noticed a tiny bump on Sophia's hand during her visit. It clearly wasn't a burn. Sophia wasn't very talkative at the time. I didn't know whether she had been abused or whether Lauryn had made up another false allegation. A few days later, I met with an investigator with the Texas Department of Family and Protective Services (TDFPS) in Dallas. I thought that this would be a simple interview to get the facts. I hadn't done anything wrong. I had been a responsible father trying to get my daughter out of what I knew to be a dangerous and hostile situation.

The investigator was a young Black female who appeared very inexperienced. The investigator asked me several probing questions.

"How was Sophia's index finger burned?" she asked.

"I was not aware of a burn," I stated.

She said that Lauryn had confirmed that while Sophia was with me, she had a "swollen throat, an ear infection, and pink-eye with mucus draining from her eye and a burn on her finger that had bubbled up." Lauryn had further stated in the report that a nine-year-old boy had "licked her butt and inserted his pe*** inside her mouth and partially inside her va****" and that Sophia had belt marks on her leg, stomach, and arms.

I almost threw up as I listened to the statements. Had Sophia been sexually abused? Was it true? By whom? I was angry and wanted to get to the bottom of it. Lauryn mentioned a lot of other explicit language, including that the young boy had "rubbed her va**** with his hand."

I told the investigator that I was not aware of a burn to her finger. She asked me about how I disciplined her. I told her that I believed in verbal discipline. I mentioned that I had once spanked her a few times on the bottom part of her legs. I told her that I was not a proponent of corporal punishment. She asked me about the babysitter for my daughter and if I was aware that she had been sexually abused by a boy eight or nine years old while in daycare. I told her that this was my first-time hearing of this.

Lauryn stated that she had also taken Sophia to have a physical examination at Medical City. I was later able to review the records from Medical City and Sophia's pediatrician as well as interviews conducted at the Child Advocacy Center. They did not show anything conclusive that any abuse had occurred. I also received a call from the detective at the Cedar Hill Police Department. He appeared suspicious about the allegations. Lauryn would not cooperate with his requests. He told me that he was concerned about the validity and authenticity of her allegations.

The TDFPS interview lasted forty-five minutes to an hour. I could tell from her line of questioning and the look on her face that she did not believe me. After the interview was over, she told me that I would receive a letter in the mail letting me know her findings. Three to four weeks later, I received a letter from TDFPS. The letter stated that there was reason to believe that neglectful supervision had occurred. I almost fainted after I received the letter.

How could this investigator arrive at such a decision? I was infuriated. I had worked for many years with children who had open cases with TDFPS. I was not a negligent father. After I received the letter, I wrote to the state and requested all documents pertaining to the investigation.

A few days later, I wrote a letter of appeal to the regional office for TDFPS based in Arlington, Texas. I included in my request for appeal medical records from Sophia's physician. I included notes from the Cedar Hill Police Department, the Child Advocacy Center, and notes from my interview with TDFPS staff and supervisors. I also included Lauryn's psychiatric evaluation. The courts, schools, law enforcement, and now TDFPS seemed to believe her! I included the following statement in my appeal of the decision:

> I have spent my entire adult life advocating on the behalf of children and youth involved in the juvenile justice, child welfare and mental health systems in Texas and nationally. I have worked with TDFPS on several cases in the past 14 years in my professional life. I work for an agency that has managed TDFPS contracts in North Texas. I know the system thoroughly. This is not just my vocation; it is my avocation as well. I have fought to get to see my daughter, even after Lauryn filed false charges against me.

> When my daughter was just one year old, Lauryn stated that she feared that I would sexually abuse my own daughter. How long will this injustice occur? There is a child involved here who is being used as a pawn to hurt me so that I can never see her again. I will not stand idly by while this happens!

After I met with the regional administrators for TDFPS, the "reason to believe" disposition for neglectful supervision of Sophia had been changed to "ruled out." The state had overturned its decision. I was elated. It had taken me several weeks of research and reviewing documents and state regulations to fight this determination.

I could not believe that "system leaders" could make such mistakes. I began to wonder if I would ever achieve justice and fairness in Dallas County and in the State of Texas.

While I had won the appeal with TDFPS, I was still dealing with Judge Gaston on the custody case. I was so exhausted that I called my attorney and told her that I was willing to work out some arrangement with Lauryn. Negotiating with a person diagnosed with borderline personality disorder is painful, to say the least. They often have an inability to negotiate. It is either win or lose. We both worked through our attorneys to reach an agreement to present to Judge Gaston.

I consented for Lauryn to serve as the primary custodial parent, with us both as joint managing conservators. I would have standard unsupervised visitations on the first, third, and fifth weekends. We were to do our exchanges at a mutually agreed upon location. We were both to notify one another if either of us moved out of Dallas County. Lauryn was required to notify me of each school that Sophia attended.

I knew that none of the language in the final court order mattered to Lauryn. The only thing that mattered was that she was the custodial parent. This gave her the blank check that she so desperately wanted. She never had any intention of ever letting me see Sophia again. She didn't care about the psychological and emotional damage that this would create for Sophia. It was all about Lauryn getting her way!

After Judge Gaston awarded Lauryn primary custody, I knew that there was only a slim chance that I would ever see Sophia again on a consistent basis. Lauryn had done everything in her power to make sure that I would never get regular unsupervised visitations.

It appeared that everything that I had avoided in my childhood was resurfacing now that I had met Lauryn. I had worked hard to get an education and avoid so many of the pitfalls of so many of my family members. Now I was facing legal challenges. I had avoided the family curse of drinking heavily or using drugs. I had lost too many relatives to alcohol and drugs at an early age. I was determined not to become another statistic.

With all the personal challenges that I was facing, I continued to drink daily. I had been convicted of two misdemeanor DWIs. I had never felt that I was addicted to alcohol prior to meeting Lauryn. The drinking was making my depression worse. My therapist even considered not conducting therapy sessions with me unless I stopped drinking at least for a few days. I was not able to make that commitment at the time.

I was an emotional wreck. Crystal and I were not together. I wasn't getting to see Sophia on a regular basis. My finances were in bad shape. It was 2004, and it seemed that the life that I had worked so hard to build was coming apart at the seams. I focused on work like never before. I traveled a lot, but this didn't keep my mind off the tremendous challenges that I was facing in my personal life.

Sophia was almost four years old when Lauryn left Dallas and moved with her to Houston. I searched feverishly to contact Sophia through schools and her relatives. I hired private investigators to look for Lauryn and Sophia. Lauryn had gone underground. Investigators were not able to find her. She had used the restraining orders to act like she was the victim. Her employment and residential information were kept from the public record.

Lauryn never informed me of the moves that she made with Sophia as the final court order warranted. For her, it was always about control. If I did not give in to her demands, she would make me pay.

After Lauryn was terminated from Texas Technology, she earned her teacher certification to teach high school-level math. Lauryn was a math genius. She had used this as a guise to move back to Houston. The temporary orders from Judge Gaston had stated that the court must approve any relocation, and I must be informed in advance of such a move. Lauryn didn't follow anybody's orders, not even Judge Gaston's.

The move to Houston was discouraging. I would not get to see Sophia again on a consistent basis for many years. Judge Gaston didn't impose any consequences for Lauryn moving without the court's approval.

After Lauryn left Dallas County against the court's order, I did everything in my power to find Sophia. Through my attorney, we filed several motions for enforcement with the Harris County courts. We were never able to get Lauryn served. From late 2004 to 2009, I made several attempts to locate Sophia. I first contacted local school districts. I then targeted schools in the Houston area.

After contacting several schools at random, I finally contacted a deputy superintendent at a suburban school district outside of Houston. A few days later, I was at the school district with my certified court documents in hand. I had learned the hard way that court documents had to be certified.

I shared with the deputy superintendent my story. After a few minutes of conversation and reviewing legal documents, he told me that Sophia attended the school. He said that I had permission to meet with her. I met with the school principal, who gave me permission to visit with Sophia. I met Sophia in the school library. After several minutes, Sophia walked into the library. She wore glasses and resembled me a great deal. I was so excited to see her. She looked so different. She gave me a hug as tears streamed down my face. I knew that she had endured a lot.

I talked to her while she ate lunch. I asked her a lot about her likes and dislikes. She was not that forthcoming. I spoke with one of her teachers. Her teacher expressed a great deal of frustration dealing with Sophia. She was a good learner, yet she was hyperactive and cussed a lot in class. I knew that she had learned this from Lauryn.

Her teacher was also concerned that Lauryn was not following up on the teacher's recommendations.

I knew then that Sophia was in trouble. There was not much that I could do at the time. Through my attorney, we filed additional motions for enforcement in the Harris County courts to enforce the Dallas County order and attempted to get visitation. The most difficult challenge was getting a good physical address on Lauryn. She had used the restraining orders to not notify me of her physical address for safety reasons.

Through a private investigator, I found that Lauryn taught high school at the same school district where Lauryn attended school. Once I located the high school, I hired a local process server in Harris County. Despite several months of attempts, they were unable to serve her. Lauryn did everything in her power to not be served, including parking far away from the campus or getting a police escort for her safety. Lauryn was the one who had victimized and traumatized others, yet she was being treated like royalty.

I was just a father attempting to have a relationship with his daughter, but I was treated like a criminal. Lauryn had told the schools that I had beaten her and threatened Sophia. The school officials seemed to know that Lauryn was trouble, but they were fearful of her. Lauryn knew school policies better than most school administrators. She would write long e-mails to the school administration and board of trustees threatening a lawsuit whenever she felt that things were not going her way.

After my visits at Sophia's school a few times in the spring of 2005, Lauryn moved once again. Lauryn moved Sophia's school at least once every year. Lauryn moved so that she would not be detected. I hired another private investigator the following school year. This time, Lauryn had moved back to the Dallas area near Frisco, Texas. Frisco was an upper-income suburb northwest of Dallas. Lauryn always lived above her means. Status was extremely important to her.

I soon visited Sophia at her school in Frisco. Sophia was in elementary school. This time, I went directly to the school principal and showed them my court documents. They allowed me to visit with Sophia the same day. I met with her in the school cafeteria. She had grown a lot taller. She still wore glasses. I took a few pictures with her and shared them with my family. They were excited that I had a chance to visit with her. The schoolteachers continued to have concerns about Sophia's erratic behavior in the classroom and her academic performance. They knew that Sophia had some serious challenges at home.

I visited with Sophia several times during the school year of 2006–2007. I knew that Lauryn would move to another school district the following year. I talked to her, took pictures, and left her money. I always told her that I loved her and that I wanted to see her more often, but Lauryn was making it difficult.

I was able to visit Sophia several times throughout the school year during her lunch period. I knew that Lauryn would change schools for Sophia once I had visits with her. Frisco was a great school district for Sophia. I was concerned about her changing schools every year. It made it difficult for me to maintain a consistent relationship with her. Lauryn didn't care about any of this. For Lauryn, her primary concerns were based on her romantic relationship with Attorney Nimpson and ensuring that I did not have any contact with Sophia.

I never wanted to place Sophia in a situation where Lauryn would retaliate against her. I knew that Lauryn would take any and everything out on Sophia. Anything that went wrong was blamed on Sophia. I was also concerned that Sophia was the one caring for Lauryn. Children with parents who have borderline personality disorder often deal with a range of emotions from their parents. They often don't have healthy parent-child relationships. They grow up insecure and question themselves constantly. They also don't get their emotional needs met. This can be confusing for children when they most need caring and consistency from both parents.

After a little more than a year in Frisco, Lauryn moved back to the Houston area. I hired yet another private investigator but could not locate her. It would be over two years before I would see Sophia after she had moved from Frisco. If anything, Lauryn was always unpredictable. I continued to file motions for enforcement through my attorney in the Harris County courts. I always thought that there was a small chance that Lauryn would make a mistake and we would locate her. This time, Lauryn reached out to me. I received a call from a blocked number. It was Lauryn. She told me that they were having a big birthday celebration for Sophia, and I was invited. The birthday party would be near Houston. I was excited beyond measure.

By this time, Crystal and I had gotten back together. I told her about Lauryn's call. She was concerned about my safety. Was this a setup? She, too, was excited for me. She told me not to go to the birthday party alone. I took her counsel to heart. I asked my best friend, Reggie, to travel with me to Houston. He agreed.

I hadn't seen Sophia for over two years. I didn't know what she would be like. I was hopeful that we could spend some quality time together away from Lauryn. Lauryn had always told Sophia that I didn't want to see her. Everything was my fault. I was the bad guy who had hurt her mom and threatened to harm her.

The day finally came for me to visit with Sophia in Houston for her ninth birthday party. Reggie and I had made the four-hour trip. I told him to look out for me while I went inside to visit with Sophia. Lauryn had plotted against me so many times. My heart was racing. When we finally arrived in Houston that Saturday afternoon, I called Lauryn and told her that I was there. I went into a large entertainment complex with a lot of young people. After a few minutes of searching, Lauryn came up to me and attempted to give me a hug and introduce me to other family and friends.

Lauryn always wanted to impress other people. She acted as if we had a good relationship. After Lauryn committed heinous acts, she always acted as if nothing had happened. I didn't know if this was a game that she played, or mental illness or both. One of the people who Lauryn introduced me to was Linda Forbes, Sophia's godmother. Linda would prove to be a godsend for Sophia. I was pleased to see that there were other responsible and caring people who surrounded and supported her.

After several minutes, I finally had a chance to visit with Sophia. She never called me Dad in the presence of Lauryn. That would have afforded me too much power and influence over Sophia.

Sophia said to me, "Hi, Gerald."

There was always a bit of pain when she called me by my first name. I knew that it was Lauryn's manipulation. BPD parents often cut their children off from their other parent. It is a form of control or manipulation. The other parent was evil, depraved, and lacked any concern for their child. The child suffers most with this kind of parenting, yet it is frequently how parents with BPD parent. Some courts refer to it as *"parent alienation of affection."* Everything is about manipulation, obfuscation, and control. The child is just a pawn.

I stayed at Sophia's birthday party for a couple of hours. I was ecstatic to see her. I gave her a few gifts. Lauryn rolled out a huge bicycle that was too large for her to ride. Lauryn also showered her with other gifts since she always appeared as "super-mom." Everything was larger than life for her. Large gifts. Expensive neighborhoods. Designer clothes. The newest computers. It was all a front. Years later, Sophia told me that Lauryn took back all the toys after her birthday celebration was over and returned them to the store! It was all a show.

Before I returned to Dallas, I gave Sophia a big hug. I didn't know when I would get to see her again. I attempted to get contact information for Sophia's godmother. Lauryn made sure that we did not have an opportunity to talk to one another. She was always fearful that I might get a chance to communicate with my own daughter without her supervision and control.

After the birthday party, I made the long trek back to Dallas. I was grateful for the opportunity to see Sophia. I was thankful that nothing bad had occurred. I always expected the worst with Lauryn.

Georgia on My Mind

After Sophia's birthday party in Houston, I lost contact with her and Lauryn again for a couple of years. I hired yet another private investigator to find Lauryn's whereabouts. A breakthrough finally came with a family friend who had formerly worked in the child welfare system. They were able to find Lauryn through Brian Benson. Brian resided near Atlanta, Georgia and he was the key that we needed to find the whereabouts of Lauryn and Sophia. I didn't receive any notification from Lauryn that she was moving out of state. She never informed me of her whereabouts.

Lauryn had moved to Atlanta in 2008. She had just finished earning her master's degree from Prairie View A&M University near Houston, Texas. Despite her mental illness, she had earned her graduate degree in mathematics. She had a brilliant mind, yet she was a tortured soul. She had landed a teaching job at Maynard Holbrook Jackson High School in Atlanta as a math teacher.

Leaving Texas meant that Lauryn didn't have to worry about my visits with Sophia and the court's orders. At least, that was what Lauryn thought. She didn't know that I would turn over every stone to find Sophia.

Brian had been arrested on assault charges. Lauryn wanted Brian to buy her a new car. She knew that he was wealthy and had played in the NFL. Brian was reluctant to buy Lauryn a new vehicle. They had only known one another for a few months. Lauryn was determined to get him to buy her a new SUV. After Brian refused, Lauryn said that Brian had assaulted her. After he was released from jail, she told him that she would drop the charges only if he gave her money to buy a new SUV. Brian gave her $5, 000 towards payment on a used SUV.

Attorney Nimpson worked with Lauryn to extort Brian out of his money. The charges were dismissed.

Prior to meeting Lauryn, Brian Benson didn't have an arrest history. Brian had played in the NFL as a tight end. He stood 6 feet, 6 inches tall and weighed over 240 pounds. Most importantly for Lauryn, he had several rental properties throughout the greater Atlanta area. She had a knack for dating men with money. Brian was not the only man who had played in the NFL whom Lauryn dated.

Lauryn always dated men who were financially stable. They were typically married and had a lot to lose. She knew that the men she dated couldn't afford to get arrested or they would lose their jobs and reputations. She always targeted the men's girlfriends or wives.

Attorney Nimpson was willing to go to any extent to help Lauryn. He was not licensed to practice law in Georgia, but he did his best to help her anyway. I always felt that she had threatened to report his unethical behavior to the State Bar of Texas if he did not continue to help her. Lauryn often used threats, bribes, extortion, and even physical violence to intimidate her victims. She was always one step ahead. She had learned to survive in the streets of Chicago. If nothing else, Lauryn was a survivor.

In Atlanta, Lauryn was a sought-after educator. She was a math genius. She knew how to present herself both to prospective employers and to the men she dated.

Lauryn had her eye on Brian after she met him at Maynard Jackson during her first week of employment.

Lauryn first approached Brian after the school day ended. Lauryn knew he was a computer instructor. She asked him to help her with her computer. He did not know at the time that Lauryn was an engineer and knew more about computers than he did. Lauryn used this opportunity to make a pass at Brian and let him know that she had an interest in him. She saw his wedding ring, but that did not mean anything to her.

That same evening, Lauryn intentionally left her keys at his desk. As she sauntered back in to get them, Lauryn reached up and gave Brian a kiss. That kiss started a love affair that would last for many years. Brian didn't know the danger that he was in. Once Lauryn became involved with a man, she often became obsessive.

Within a matter of days, Lauryn had a romantic tryst with Brian in the school building. Lauryn knew that other teachers at Maynard Jackson were interested in Brian. She quickly let them know that Brian was "her man." On several occasions, Lauryn had altercations with teachers that led to the principal becoming involved.

Lauryn would soon let Brian's wife, Sandy, know about the affair. Sandy taught special-needs kids in Atlanta. She loved Brian beyond measure. Within a matter of weeks, Lauryn was calling and texting Sandy. She had hoped that this would cause Brian's wife to leave him so that she could have Brian all to herself. She did not know that Brian had a long history of affairs with other women. Sandy knew about these affairs. She had hoped that Brian would grow past this phase. Sandy didn't know at the time that she was in danger. Lauryn didn't make idle threats.

I finally reached out to Brian over e-mail and he responded a few days later. I was afraid that he wouldn't speak with me about Lauryn. I told him that I was Sophia's biological father. Brian said that he had encouraged Lauryn to allow me to see Sophia.

"She made you out to be a monster, man," Brian intoned.

I told him that I knew that he had been arrested. I told him my story of the many false reports against me.

Brian said, "She did the same sh** to you that she did to me. She needs to get some help, man."

Brian always talked about getting Lauryn help. I told him that she was diagnosed with borderline personality disorder, schizoaffective and narcissistic personality disorder. I asked him about Sophia.

Brian said, "I try and talk Lauryn into letting you see Sophia. I told her that Sophia needs her dad."

I asked Brian to send me some pictures of Sophia.

I spoke with Brian again the next day. He sent me a few pictures of Sophia. She had grown a lot since I last saw her in Houston. The smile couldn't disguise the deep sadness that I saw in her eyes. She was tall, thin, and wore braids. Brian also shared with me that Lauryn often mistreated Sophia.

Brian said, "One time, Lauryn knocked Sophia over the couch with her fist for nothing. Sophia was bleeding from her mouth. I told Lauryn that I would leave her if she ever did that again."

Brian also told me about another incident when Lauryn had forced Sophia to pick up her feces out of the toilet and smear it all over her face. Lauryn had threatened her class that she would do the same thing to them if they did not obey her. After this story, I immediately filed a report with the Georgia Division of Family and Children Services (DFCS) in Atlanta.

My experience in other states with the child welfare system was that investigations were either not taken seriously or the system would overreact and remove the child. In my case, I was never able to get the child welfare system to conduct a thorough investigation.

I had now filed reports in the Texas and Georgia child welfare systems. Thorough investigations were never conducted in either state.

After I realized that Sophia was in danger, I further resolved to find Sophia and take Lauryn to court. I had heard many people say that Georgia was a "Daddy State," and Texas was a "Momma State." Georgia was known to give men a fair shot at custody.

By the fall of 2011, I was in Atlanta searching for an attorney to represent me. After a couple of days of interviews, I didn't feel good about my prospects. On the second day, I passed by a law firm en route to the airport and went in to meet with the attorney. Her name was Dorothy Lester. I was impressed with her legal experience. She seemed to care about my story. Her fees were quite high, but I knew that she was the right person to represent me in Georgia. I signed an agreement with her before I left for the airport.

I felt really good after I had retained an attorney in Atlanta. Within a few months, I had gone from locating Brian Benson, Lauryn, and Sophia to securing an attorney.

As the saying goes, "It wasn't the beginning of the end, but it was at least the end of the beginning." I came back home to Dallas excited. I felt good just knowing where Sophia lived. She was in school in Alpharetta, Georgia, an upper-income area outside Atlanta, Georgia.

Brian and I were speaking with one another a few times each week. He finally shared with me Lauryn's place of employment. He told me that she was now a math teacher at North Atlanta High School, located in the Buckhead area of Atlanta. Sophia attended middle school in Alpharetta, Georgia. She was in the sixth grade.

How could Lauryn get a prime teaching job at one of the premier schools in Georgia with all her challenges? She had a gift for convincing people that she was a great teacher and humanitarian. She knew how to use her charm to her advantage. She could cry or laugh, whatever the occasion called for. She didn't mind sleeping her way to the top or just to get in the door.

I shared all this information with my attorney. We agreed on a legal strategy. We would get the Texas order domesticated in Georgia. We would then file for a motion for enforcement so that I could get visitations with Sophia in Georgia. If Lauryn refused to allow me to have visitations, we could fight for custody. I thought that it was a winning strategy. We first had to get Lauryn served.

On the Battlefield

It had been an exhausting three months, yet I felt encouraged. My church family was praying for us. Since 2008, I had stopped drinking alcohol and had become an assistant pastor at a small progressive church in Fort Worth, Texas. I felt better than I had in many years. After I stopped drinking, the depression and anxiety went away. I was ready for whatever battles lay ahead.

I continued to travel a lot with my job. I was concerned that Lauryn would attempt to harm my family while I was out of town. Crystal was rightfully concerned. Megan and Moriah were terrified of Lauryn. They had heard horror stories about her for many years. My in-laws were concerned for our safety as well. I always said to them, "God has a hedge of protection around us." I was convinced that I could not fight for children across the United States and not fight to save my own daughter.

Brian Benson had already helped us a great deal. I also received a surprising call from Attorney Nimpson. He told me that he wanted to meet and talk with me. I was floored! Attorney Nimpson had done so much to harm my family. He had helped Lauryn to file false affidavits against Crystal and me for many years. Now he wanted to help us. I knew that he was extremely unethical and would do anything to help Lauryn.

A few days later, I met with Attorney Nimpson for lunch at Pappas restaurant in Dallas. I was very cautious. I didn't know what to expect from him. We shook hands and began to discuss why he wanted to meet with me.

I was surprised when Attorney Nimpson said: "I am sorry for how I worked against you. I want you to get to see Sophia. She needs you. Man, if I were you, I would move to a gated community where

Lauryn can't find you. She wants to kill you. She will do anything. I got caught up with Lauryn. I wanted to help you, but I couldn't. Just be careful. Lauryn has plans to leave Georgia since you are on her trail. She is going to move to a small town and change her name and identity or leave the country. She is fluent in Japanese and will probably move to Japan. She already has passports for her and Sophia."

I was stunned. Was Lauryn was going to leave Atlanta? Was she going to flee to Japan? Attorney Nimpson and I would continue to talk for several weeks. He must have felt a deep sense of guilt for all the harm that he had done to our family. He shared with me Lauryn's every move.

Lauryn was fluent in Japanese. Why Japanese? I was never able to figure it out. Lauryn was a genius. She had a mastery of languages, math, and theater. Yet she was unstable. She was violent. She was a threat to herself and others.

I shared this information with Attorney Lester. I couldn't believe what I had heard. I didn't talk to Attorney Nimpson for several weeks. He called me once again after we started having court hearings in Georgia. I always knew that he was looking out for Lauryn's best interest. At least he was providing me with useful information.

Attorney Nimpson had gone to extreme lengths on behalf of Lauryn. His license to practice law in Texas had been suspended. I believe that this was in part due to the many unethical activities that he had done. He would still do anything to help her. Lauryn always found men who would go to great extremes to rescue her at any cost. Attorney Nimpson was one of them. He had been Lauryn's lover and lawyer for over ten years. A short time after our last conversation, Attorney Nimpson told me that we had to cease communicating. I wasn't surprised.

I was grateful that he had shared some pertinent information with me. Attorney Nimpson and Brian Benson had both helped me a great deal. They were both smitten by Lauryn. They couldn't leave her clutches.

After my conversations with Attorney Nimpson, I knew that I had to move with haste before Lauryn went on the run. Lauryn had been on the run for many years now.

Brian shared with me a lot of critical information about what Lauryn was doing harm to Sophia. Lauryn often told Sophia, "I will kill you so that I can start a new family." Sophia believed her. Lauryn didn't just make idle threats. She was so impulsive. She had severe mood swings. She was violent one moment and acted like a child the next. Any small disruption would send Lauryn into a state of rage. Sophia bore the brunt of her rage.

Brian shared with me that Lauryn slapped Sophia in the face with a belt until she bled. She would then keep her home from school so that nobody would know about the abuse.

Lauryn thought through her every action. She made sure that nobody saw the scars from the years of whippings on every part of Sophia's body. Once, Linda Forbes was helping Sophia to put on a bathing suit. She noticed the scars on Sophia's body. When Lauryn saw this, she quickly stopped Linda from helping her. She did not want Linda to see the welts and scars that she had inflicted on Sophia.

Lauryn's family knew that she was abusive to Sophia. They refused to say anything. Lauryn was the only one who had made it out of "the hood" as far as they were concerned. They were fearful that Lauryn would lash out and never speak to them again. Lauryn supplied them with money. They chose money over Sophia's safety!

The only person to really confront Lauryn about the abuse was Linda Forbes. She had confronted Lauryn several times about her treatment of Sophia. She did it in such a way that Lauryn would not shut her out. She wanted to be there for Sophia. Had Linda gone to the authorities, Lauryn would have severed their relationship. There was always hell to pay when you crossed Lauryn! Lauryn demanded blind loyalty. You either supported her or you were the enemy.

Brian had told me numerous stories about Lauryn mistreating Sophia. Once, Sophia went to Lauryn's room while Brian was there. Lauryn ripped her robe off and said, "You're probably a whore sleeping around with men."

Sophia was only eight or nine years of age. Sophia walked away with her head hung low. Sophia was always "a whore and b****."

Ages eight to eleven were Sophia's toughest years. Lauryn's mental illness appeared to worsen over time. She was deteriorating emotionally and psychologically. There were times in which Lauryn was jealous of Sophia. She would always say to Sophia, "Brian is my man."

Lauryn physically abused Sophia most of the time. Sophia would often go to school with long-sleeved sweaters, even when it was hot outside. Lauryn didn't want Sophia to interact with other children or adults. She was fearful that they would find out about the abuse.

Lauryn would often act out different characters while she beat Sophia unmercifully. She would sometimes act like Barney the Purple Dinosaur and rub her stomach and call her "b**** and ho." She would oftentimes enter Sophia's room in the dark. Sophia knew her footsteps. When she entered the room, she would be cussing at Sophia and the beating would resume. Lauryn often talked about killing her and throwing her body parts in different states.

"I will send your head to Texas and your other body parts throughout Georgia," Lauryn often said.

Lauryn was psychotic almost every day. When Sophia was not the victim, it was a student in class or an innocent bystander. The only time that she seemed to be sane and sensible was when Brian was present.

Lauryn didn't have any sense of appropriate boundaries with Sophia or the men she dated. Lauryn always put her relationships with men before Sophia. When men were around, Sophia did not get much attention. Lauryn would often spend days with her boyfriend while Sophia was at home alone. During these times, she would call her godmother, Linda Forbes. On more than one occasion, Linda threatened Lauryn that she would report her to CPS if Lauryn continued to leave her at home alone.

On one occasion, Sophia had answered the door in shorts. Brian was at the door. Lauryn suddenly became enraged. Lauryn yelled to Sophia, "Brian is my man. What do you want him to do? Do you want him to stick his fat d*** in you're a**?" Lauryn slapped her several times and told her to go to her room.

Lauryn's personal life was in chaos. She was moving to a different home almost every year to avoid being detected. She owed the

IRS in back taxes to the tune of over $70,000. This did not include student loans totaling over $60,000. On the surface, everything looked good. Lauryn lived in very expensive neighborhoods. She wore the right clothes and went to Starbucks every day. Yet she lived a life full of despair.

Sophia, meanwhile, lived a life of isolation and desperation. Lauryn never allowed her to play with other children. She was Lauryn's rag doll, punching bag, robot, and paycheck. Lauryn always made sure that Sophia looked like the average suburban child. Yet, those who knew her knew that something was wrong. They knew that Sophia was being mistreated.

Sophia had been choked and sat upon by Lauryn numerous times. Sophia once woke up tied up in black plastic bags that had been tied at both ends. She started to kick and scream. After numerous attempts, she worked her way out of the bag.

Sophia immediately bolted out of the door and ran down the stairs. Lauryn ran down the stairs after her. Sophia threatened to call the cops if she ever did this again. Lauryn tried talking her out of it. Lauryn said, "Baby, Momma's sorry. I will never do this again." Lauryn never kept her word.

Lauryn also sat on Sophia's chest when she was frustrated with her. Sophia gasped for air and foamed at the mouth. While sitting on her, Lauryn yelled, "Now get up b****."

Lauryn wouldn't allow Sophia to call me during the holidays. Lauryn knew that Sophia would tell her story if allowed contact with me. Periodically, Lauryn would visit her family in Chicago. They had witnessed some of Lauryn's abusive whipping of Sophia, but nobody stood up for Sophia.

In the fall of 2011, I finally visited Sophia's school in Alpharetta, GA, the week before school was out for winter break. I was excited to visit with her. I went to her school bearing Christmas gifts. I went to the attendance clerk and told her that I was Sophia's father. I handed her a certified copy of the Texas court order. She then asked me to be seated. I was then met by the school principal and counselor. They had frozen looks on their faces. The counselor was crying. They told me that they were sorry, but I could not visit with Sophia. They had called the central administration and were informed that Lauryn had given them orders for me not to visit with Sophia.

I asked them how Sophia was doing in school. They said in no uncertain terms that Sophia was in trouble and that Lauryn was exceedingly difficult to deal with. I told them that I was filing legal documents so that I could have visitations with Sophia. They strongly encouraged me to do so. The counselor asked that I help Sophia with her emotional distress. She cried as we talked about Sophia's needs.

I felt dejected as I left Sophia's school. I knew that she was suffering in silence. The principal and counselor were doing their best to help her. I was looking forward to the New Year.

New Year

I celebrated the New Year with great anticipation. Attorney Lester was working to get the Texas orders domesticated in Georgia and ensure that I had my visitations enforced. I wasn't confident that Lauryn would ever comply with the court's orders. She had a long history of defying court orders in Texas.

Our initial challenge was to get Lauryn served legal documents. Lauryn was masterful at evading being served. I was attempting to have Lauryn served at North Atlanta High School. To evade being served, she parked several blocks away from the school to avoid being detected. The process server hid under her vehicle and served her as she opened her door.

He notified her that she had been served by the Superior Court of Fulton County, State of Georgia, Family Division. We were excited. We had finally had her served. The court date was set for January 12 before Judge Dempsey. I had arrived in town the night before so that I could make the early morning meeting.

Attorney Lester and I did not think that Lauryn would show up for the hearing. As my attorney and I awaited the court hearing before Judge Dempsey, Lauryn slowly sauntered off the elevators. As always, she brought with her several boxes of legal papers. She had always done this to intimidate me.

The family court system appeared to operate differently in Georgia than in Texas. Lauryn and I were not sitting far apart from one another as we waited for court to begin. Lauryn mean-mugged me the entire time. After what seemed like an eternity, we entered the court. Judge Dempsey was sitting at the head of the table, and Lauryn and I were sitting across from one another. Judge Dempsey called the court to order. She was a stern-looking White woman who appeared to be in her late thirties or early forties.

Judge Dempsey asked, "Are you represented by an attorney, Ms. Burns?"

Lauryn responded, "No."

Judge Dempsey then asked Lauryn a series of questions about her ability to retain an attorney. Lauryn was bringing home almost $70,000 a year as a math teacher in Georgia. In addition, she was receiving over $1,300 a month for child support payments from me. She was also extorting money from Brian Benson. She could afford a private attorney.

My attorney then presented the domestication order and motion for enforcement. As she did so, Lauryn kept interrupting the judge. Judge Dempsey asked her to "be quiet" several times. After several interruptions, she called for the bailiff to be present inside the courtroom throughout the hearing. Judge Dempsey began to see Lauryn's mental illness on full display. After Attorney Lester had presented her information, Judge Dempsey allowed Lauryn to speak.

Lauryn presented a long, rambling letter that Sophia had allegedly written. Lauryn often wrote long letters and signed Sophia's name to them. It was apparent that the letter was not written by Sophia. Lauryn began to talk about how I had been violent towards her. She mentioned the restraining orders in Texas and the previous charges filed against me.

Lauryn informed the court that I drank alcohol in the presence of Sophia. She told Judge Dempsey that I had been convicted of DWIs in Texas. She provided Judge Dempsey a copy of the letter from the Texas Department of Family and Protective Services showing that there was reason to believe that neglectful supervision had occurred. Lauryn didn't know that the State of Texas had overturned the neglectful supervision ruling.

Lauryn shared the history of violence against her and the history of restraining orders. Judge Dempsey carefully listened to her presentation.

Lauryn presented a typed letter allegedly written by Sophia:

> I heard that you found out that I stay in Georgia. It makes me hesitate to answer do I want to stay with you or not. Last time I was with you we had many bad memories to bring back. Even though this was so-called eight years ago it was very traumatizing. I trusted you then, but now trust has faded away. If you want me to bring back some of my worst memories, I will refresh your memory. When I was two, I remember you were drunk driving. All I saw was flashing lights pulling you over. I remember when I was hurt in a very bad way because of you. You didn't help the police find the answers. All you did was to protect your best friend and his son. I am worried about getting raped.

The letter was signed January 11, 2012. Lauryn had included a picture of Sophia. Lauryn always raised the specter of Sophia being raped. I had never consumed alcohol in Sophia's presence. I had abstained from alcohol altogether since 2008. Lauryn also submitted a motion for continuance and a motion for supervised visitation. Lauryn had signed both motions. The motions appeared to be written by Lauryn and Attorney Nimpson. Although Attorney Nimpson was not licensed to practice law in Georgia, he helped Lauryn to prepare legal documents.

I shared with Judge Dempsey that I had not drunk alcohol since August 2008. I told her about my DWI history. I had completed outpatient treatment to address my alcohol addiction in 2008. The judge listened intently. I also shared with her certified legal documents from the Texas Department of Family and Protective Services stating the neglectful supervision determination had been overturned. I shared with the judge my history of helping to improve the lives of troubled young people nationally. My testimony removed any concerns that Judge Dempsey had about my background.

Lauryn could not believe that Judge Dempsey was not falling for her antics. The Georgia courts were not reacting to the false allegations that Lauryn had made in Dallas County. It was a new day in Georgia!

Judge Dempsey ordered that I have an initial reunification with Sophia in Alpharetta, Georgia, on that same day at 7:00 p.m. at a Chili's restaurant. I would have one to two hours of unsupervised time with Sophia.

Judge Dempsey further ordered that Lauryn release school records to me and allow visitation at her school. I was scheduled to have a second visit with Sophia on a weekend to be worked out between both parties. The visitation was to occur from 12:00 p.m. to 8:00 p.m. on a Saturday and 10:00 a.m. to 4:00 p.m. on a Sunday. I walked out of court with a sense of victory. We finally had a judge who was fair and willing to listen to the facts and merits of the case from both parties. As court was adjourned, Lauryn walked out of court visibly shaken.

After court, we arranged a meeting at Chili's in Alpharetta as Judge Dempsey had ordered. Lauryn had a puzzled look on her face. I didn't know if she would run or just not show up. I immediately went to Chili's to wait on Lauryn and Sophia. I knew that all this was unsettling to her. I didn't know how she would respond. Lauryn had always won in Texas family courts. I could feel that the outcome would be different in Georgia. Lauryn couldn't deal with defeat or loss.

I sat in the parking lot at Chili's for a couple of hours waiting for Lauryn and Sophia. Lauryn finally arrived after 7:00 p.m. She was an hour late. I watched her as she walked into the restaurant with Sophia. Sophia had a backpack on her shoulders. Her hair was in braids and she wore glasses. I entered the door behind her. When I saw her, my eyes welled up with tears.

The waiter seated us at a booth. Lauryn always presented herself as super-mom. Lauryn told Sophia to call her if she needed help and to work on her homework while sitting there with me. I sat across from her and asked her how she was doing.

Sophia said "I am doing okay, Gerald. Why don't you just wait until I am an adult, and I will make up my own mind to see you?"

I didn't respond for a minute. I knew that Lauryn had told her what to say. I told Sophia that I wanted to see her while she was still a child. I wanted to be involved in her life.

I had mixed emotions. I knew that Lauryn would retaliate against Sophia if she called me Dad or expressed any interest in having a positive relationship with me. I knew that she didn't want to see me out of fear. I also knew that Lauryn didn't want anybody to be close to Sophia so they wouldn't find out about the abuse. She also didn't want to lose the child support check. While it wasn't important to me, it was everything to her.

I wasn't surprised at Sophia's comments. She had to follow Lauryn's every command, or there would be grave consequences. Most of the time, Sophia was doing her homework. I didn't want to interrupt her. It was awkward. I knew that Lauryn was listening to our every word. She was probably recording our conversation. After an hour, Lauryn came back and told Sophia that she had to do more homework and get ready for bed. I gave Sophia a hug and said goodbye.

I then headed to the airport. I hoped and prayed that Lauryn would not punish Sophia for meeting with me. That was a risk that I was willing to take. I knew that she was already being abused. It was a long flight back to Dallas, but at least things were moving in the right direction.

Glimmer of Hope

We were making progress in Georgia. Lauryn thought that I would never be able to find her and Sophia. She didn't know that I would never give up on my daughter.

By the grace of God, the court proceedings were going well. I didn't think that Lauryn would appear at the court hearing or at Chili's in Alpharetta, GA as Judge Dempsey had ordered. Over the next several weeks, Lauryn and I exchanged e-mails to arrange for the next visit with Sophia in Alpharetta. As usual, Lauryn made it difficult.

Attorney Lester encouraged me to do everything in my power to communicate with Lauryn. I did so by e-mail several times. Each time, Lauryn would cuss me out and send a list of reasons why I should not have an unsupervised visit with Sophia.

I anticipated that Lauryn would give an excuse not to show up for the visitation. Lauryn had pushed hard in court for me to have supervised visitations with Sophia since I had not visited with her for a few years. I had done my best to contact Sophia by phone as Judge Dempsey had ordered, but Lauryn prevented me from doing so. We agreed on the dates of exchange to be on February 25 and 26 at North Point Mall in Alpharetta, Georgia.

Crystal traveled with me to Atlanta for the visitation. We arrived the night before. We were both nervous. We didn't know whether Lauryn would set us up or do something to harm us. Lauryn had a history of making a scene in public.

Prior to the visit, I had sent several e-mails to Lauryn to clarify the pickup location. Once I had arrived in Atlanta, Lauryn refused to respond to my e-mails and texts. Lauryn finally responded to my e-mails on Saturday, February 25 at 9:00 a.m. Lauryn always responded on her terms. Lauryn said in the e-mail:

> Your visitation will be supervised. The Fulton County Court Families First Agency will provide the supervision. Please contact them to complete your registration process in the near future. Mr. Moton will be the supervisor for this visit and has assured me that he will observe the visit, providing you with the reasonable space to visit with Sophia. The meeting times will be Saturday at noon and Sunday afternoon. I will cease all further communication with you temporarily, as you have provided an attack on both my child and myself. I will reject your efforts to proceed in such a maladaptive approach. The sole focus should be on the rebuilding a broken relationship with Sophia and not attacking me.

Once again, Lauryn had not followed Judge Dempsey's orders. She had ordered unsupervised visits with Sophia. Lauryn took the law into her own hands.

I arrived at the North Point Mall an hour early. Crystal and I walked around the mall as we waited for Lauryn and Sophia to arrive. As the time came closer for Lauryn to appear, I sat in the food court while Crystal was upstairs. I had a flashback of the Valley View Mall incident in Dallas several years earlier.

I thought about the years that I had missed with Sophia. I thought about how sad Sophia had looked the last time that I saw her in January.

Finally, I saw Lauryn appear out of the corner of my eye. Sophia was with her, along with a gentleman who looked like an older version of Malcolm X. He said that he was there to conduct a supervised visit. I told him that the court had not ordered a supervised visit. He simply proceeded to stand near me and watch my every move. He acted as if I was going to run with Sophia.

After some heated exchanges, I attempted to engage Sophia in some small talk. She was incredibly nervous. I asked her if she was hungry.

Sophia said, "Yes."

I then started to walk her over to get some pizza. We were still in the food court area. As I started to walk with Sophia to get some pizza, the gentleman with Lauryn jumped up and grabbed Sophia and said that she could not leave with me. The pizza shop was only a few feet away.

I almost blew it at that moment. Who was he? What was his real intent? Was this another one of Lauryn's lovers who would do her bidding? Was this another one of the men that Lauryn was sleeping with to get favors?

I told him in no uncertain terms, "This is my daughter, and I do not have supervised visitation. I can take my daughter with me as I please. I do not need your permission."

I had started to raise my voice and other people began to hear the conversation. Crystal was sitting not too far away. I sent her a text and told her to come back and become a witness. As Crystal approached, Lauryn began to record Crystal and called her b**** several times. Lauryn continued yelling, "b****" as she continued to record Crystal's every movement. Crystal began to record the scene on her cell phone as well.

As Lauryn continued to record Crystal, I gave Sophia a hug and told her that I would see her soon. I told Crystal that it was time to leave. Crystal stood her ground the entire time. She had been the victim of Lauryn more than once. She could have gone to prison for many years for the attempted vehicular homicide charges that Lauryn had filed against her in Texas. I considered calling the police to get the order enforced, but I didn't want to traumatize Sophia any further.

Crystal and I went back to the hotel room and sent Attorney Lester an e-mail about what had occurred. I told her that things would only get worse and that Lauryn would probably attempt to file false charges against me.

The next morning, I received a long e-mail from Lauryn. She said that she had showed up at the food court at North Point Mall at twelve noon as the court had ordered.

Lauryn wrote:

> Sophia and I, along with a number of individuals that observed us from afar for our own safety, showed up at the mall in the food court at 12 noon. We were on time today! I involved a number of people because I know how mental you are. I recorded it all and others have pictures and video to note the time. You are a liar and a manipulative man, Gerald. Your lies, ill commands and mentally unstable perceptions leave me in shock. I wish you would really focus on building your relationship with Sophia.

Lauryn had a pattern. She would always make everyone else out to be the ones who were at fault. She had done this for many years. I knew the routine. I also knew how she would ask me a series of questions about Sophia. Lauryn posed a series of questions:

> Be honest with yourself, Gerald, who is Sophia? What is her favorite color? What is her favorite meal? What makes her happy? What's her favorite song? What song will stop her in her tracks when she hears it? Who are her friends? Who is her favorite relative? What is her favorite place to visit and why? What is most important to her in her life? Her favorite sport? How many instruments can she play? Name them. What touches her heart? What are her dreams? What does she fear most in life? What does she sound like when she laughs? What makes her smile? What irritates her the most? What gives her joy? What are her favorite bible verses? What is the

best thing about church? What does she like to wear to feel comfortable on the weekends and during school? Name one item that is a must that she can't go without in her purse. What causes her to get sick? What is she allergic to? What type of soap must she use daily? What lotion must she always use? What is her favorite toothpaste? What is her favorite perfume? What is her favorite saying? What is her favorite subject in school?

Lauryn knew that she hadn't allowed me enough visits with Sophia to know the answers to these questions. How could I know such answers if I didn't get to spend time with Sophia?

I could not wait for the next court hearing. I knew that Judge Dempsey would be upset that her orders were not followed. The next status conference hearing was held before Judge Dempsey on March 16, 2012. The judge had asked for Lauryn to have Sophia present. We were scheduled to have a mediation hearing that morning and appear in court that afternoon at 2:00 p.m.

I arrived for mediation early that morning. Lauryn did not show up on time for the mediation as usual. We had mediation in Texas with a clinical psychologist that had not gone well. I knew that this one would not turn out well either.

I sat and talked to the mediator until Lauryn arrived thirty or forty-five minutes later. The mediator met with each of us separately and then together. Lauryn blamed me for everything that had gone wrong. The mediator attempted to keep the mediation positive so that we could achieve some meaningful results. After less than an hour of mediation, the mediator said that we had reached an impasse. She would inform the court of the outcome.

Lauryn told the mediator that she was biased and was being paid for by us. Lauryn always said that I had a lot of money and had bought people off. She made this reference during our initial court hearing. Judge Dempsey simply dismissed her inferences.

Lauryn once again appeared in Judge Dempsey's court that afternoon without an attorney. Judge Dempsey reviewed the previous order and asked for an update from both parties. Attorney Lester shared with the judge the challenges in my having an unsupervised visitation in February and my inability to speak with Sophia as the court had ordered. I was still not listed on the school records. Lauryn had not cooperated with the mediation. Judge Dempsey was most upset about the supervised visitation. Judge Dempsey had ordered that the visit could be unsupervised.

Judge Dempsey asked Lauryn why Sophia was not present in court as the judge had requested. Lauryn mentioned that Sophia was at a camp in Michigan. Judge Dempsey was livid. Lauryn had not received permission from the court nor informed me about this decision. The judge then pulled out a landline phone and asked Lauryn to call the camp in Michigan so that she could speak with Sophia. Lauryn scrambled to find the number.

After several minutes rummaging through her purse, Lauryn blurted out, "Your Honor, Sophia is not at a camp in Michigan. She is here in Atlanta at a friend's house."

There was complete silence in the court. I looked back and forth at my attorney and the judge. None of us could believe what we had just heard. I assumed that Lauryn had just perjured herself. She had done so many times before with no consequences. With great consternation, Judge Dempsey asked Lauryn to contact the persons who were keeping Sophia immediately. The judge threatened to confine her in the county jail if Sophia did not appear in court that afternoon. The judge adjourned the court while we waited for Sophia to arrive.

While I was waiting in the hallway, Lauryn attempted to speak with me.

"Gerald, please work with me, and let's help our daughter, please."

I could not believe it. Lauryn always acted humble when she was desperate. The minute that she received what she wanted, she would go back to her normal ways. Everything to her was an act, a show. She did whatever she thought would please the court. She would appear in court wearing a large visible cross. She had Sophia wearing various Christian symbols. Lauryn could not care less about religion. As always, she was brilliant at conforming to her environment. It had worked to her advantage for many years. She thought that it would help her to curry favor with the judge.

A couple of hours later, Lauryn appeared back in court with Sophia. The judge asked to meet with Sophia alone. After meeting for a few minutes with Sophia, Judge Dempsey said that I could spend time with Sophia and take her with me to the Atlanta airport so that we could visit. Lauryn could then pick her up once she and I had an opportunity to visit that afternoon. Lauryn had a look of disbelief on her face. The judge further ordered Lauryn to comply with the court's order.

Attorney Lester asked Judge Dempsey to have Lauryn held in contempt of Judge Dempsey's court orders. Judge Dempsey refused to hold her in contempt. She knew that Lauryn was not well mentally. Our next step was to attempt to get a guardian ad litem appointed by the court and restoration of court-ordered visitation. We also planned on sharing with the court our concern that Lauryn would leave the jurisdiction and take Sophia with her.

Judge Dempsey asked me if I wanted to visit with Sophia prior to my departure back to Dallas. I told her an emphatic, "Yes." The judge also ordered the appointment of a guardian ad litem. Their role was to act in the best interest of the child.

Sophia and I walked out of court together. We had conversations about her school and basic dad-and-daughter talk. I had missed spending time with her. I had missed out on so many important events in her life. I just cherished the moment. I took the rental car back, and Sophia walked with me into the airport to get my ticket back to Dallas. During the entire time, Sophia kept looking at her phone. I knew that Lauryn was texting her the entire time. It was all about control to Lauryn.

Sophia walked with me inside the Atlanta airport. I knew that Lauryn believed that Judge Dempsey had given me permission to take Sophia back with me to Dallas. After a few nervous minutes inside the terminal, I walked Sophia outside to meet her mom. I told Sophia that I would be calling her. I gave her a big hug, and she got into the car with Lauryn and another woman that I had never met.

"I love you, Sophia," I told her as she got into the car with Lauryn.

I sat on the plane back to Dallas in great disbelief. Judge Dempsey had ordered the appointment of a guardian ad litem. We were pleased with the developments. For once, Lauryn was not having her way in the courts.

On the Run

The appointment of a guardian ad litem was a major victory for us. We felt that the wheels of justice were finally beginning to move in our favor. Judge Dempsey appointed Attorney Winston as the guardian ad litem in our case.

Attorney Winston had several years of experience dealing with high-conflict custody battles. She was no-nonsense and could deal with Lauryn's antics. She was appointed to determine the best interests of Sophia, including awarding temporary or permanent custody. The courts were beginning to see many of the concerns that I had been raising over the past ten years.

Lauryn fought the appointment of Attorney Winston. Lauryn filed a motion to set aside the order. She sent the motion to Judge Dempsey's staff. This was the second motion that Lauryn had filed a motion "pro se," without an attorney. Since Lauryn didn't have Attorney Nimpson representing her, she was lost.

Attorney Winston was in contact with me immediately. I sent her several pages of documents and responded to all her questions and interrogatories. I scheduled a time for her to visit me at my home in Cedar Hill, Texas. She was very careful to only talk about the case. She spent two days meeting with me, my wife, and my family. She discussed with me a parenting plan and other pertinent issues.

It seemed that I was finally dealing with professionals who really cared about children. In Dallas, Lauryn knew how to manipulate the legal system (courts, prosecutors, police, etc.). Lauryn wasn't manipulating the Georgia court system the way that she had done in Texas.

A new court date was set for May 29 at 11:30 a.m. in Judge Dempsey's court. Prior to the court date, I had made multiple attempts to call Sophia on most school days and weekends after 7:00

p.m. as Judge Dempsey had ordered. Sophia did not answer her phone. The few times that she did answer, I was on speakerphone so that Lauryn could hear the entire conversation. I kept detailed notes on each day that I had attempted to speak with Sophia. I contacted Lauryn a few times via e-mail, but she responded with anger and hostility.

Attorney Winston was concerned that Lauryn had not complied with the requests for information that Judge Dempsey had ordered. Lauryn always seemed to appear combative. She was especially agitated with Attorney Winston. Lauryn had already cussed and threatened Attorney Winston. The court became increasingly concerned about Lauryn's mental instability.

During the court hearing on May 29, Lauryn mentioned to the judge that she would be visiting her family in Houston, Texas, from June 12 to July 4. The judge ordered that I pick Sophia up in Houston on June 15 at the Cheesecake Factory at the Galleria Mall in Houston and keep her until June 17. I was also ordered to have another visit from July 1 to August 6. A status hearing would be held on August 7. An initial status conference would be held on June 10.

Lauryn had always run when things were difficult. Lauryn had been on the run for many years. She would take flight, but only after she had victimized and tormented others.

She had lived in multiple states: Georgia, Texas, Illinois, Arkansas, and Alabama, among others. She would always get into trouble and leave the state before charges were filed against her. At other times, she would plead for the man that she was in a relationship with to not call the police or pursue charges against her. She would often get the men to sign affidavits of non-prosecution, as I had done in Texas.

A few days later, Lauryn filed a motion in the Georgia courts to transfer the case to the Texas family courts. The motion was signed by Attorney Matthew Nimpson. Attorney Nimpson was at it again. Lauryn had filed an affidavit in Dallas County alleging that on May 29, I had threatened to cause physical harm to Sophia. She had further stated that Sophia was suffering from extreme anxiety due to emotional stress in anticipation of unsupervised visits with her father.

Lauryn was at her best when she was filing false affidavits and motions. I had feared that she would file false charges against me in Texas. She had always won in Texas. She was quickly losing ground in Georgia. She wanted to transfer jurisdiction so that Attorney Nimpson could represent her. She also thought that she could use my prior history against me. Lauryn made several severe miscalculations this time around.

After the May 29 hearing, I knew that Lauryn would be on the run. Lauryn was not teaching during the summer months, and Sophia was out of school. I knew that she would spend the summer months attempting to move the case back to Texas. Attorney Lester was working with Attorney Winston and Judge Dempsey to keep the case in Georgia and begin to have custody hearings.

Attorney Winston had informed the courts that Sophia was not safe. Judge Dempsey had continuing jurisdiction of the case while Lauryn made visits to Texas.

I traveled to Houston on June 15 to pick up Sophia in Houston as Judge Dempsey had ordered. I traveled with my family. My sister-in-law Leslie and her friend Nan showed up to lend their support. I waited over five hours to try to get my visitation with Sophia. Lauryn did not show up with Sophia as she had been ordered. Once again, my heart was broken. It was a long drive back to Dallas. I was feeling depressed, but I kept the faith. I knew that things had to get better. There had to be a bright side somewhere.

I hadn't seen or spoken with Sophia since the Atlanta court hearing in late May. I knew that Lauryn was up to something. Lauryn filed a restraining order against me in the Dallas courts on July 3. I appeared in court pro se. Attorney Nimpson represented Lauryn. Lauryn testified that I had threatened to do harm to Sophia and caused her severe emotional distress. I was not an attorney. I could not cross-examine her. I did manage to ask Lauryn a few questions. Attorney Nimpson objected to most of them. I was out of my league.

The judge asked the three of us to meet in her chambers. I shared with the judge the proceedings in Fulton County, Georgia. She agreed to contact Judge Dempsey and to issue temporary orders. The judge ordered that Sophia have an assessment conducted by

Dallas County staff to determine if physical or emotional abuse had occurred. I was ordered to have supervised visits with Sophia until the case was resolved.

Lauryn had effectively made the case for a Dallas court to hear the case. Lauryn had given the court a Collin County address. She had given the court Attorney Nimpson's physical address. Lauryn was a permanent resident of Alpharetta, Georgia.

I could not believe that the Dallas County courts were open to hearing the case. Georgia had continuing jurisdiction. The Dallas judge had read all the proceedings in Georgia. She knew that a guardian ad litem had been appointed. I could not believe that the judge was ordering supervised visitation.

Judge Dempsey had requested a status conference to get an update on the Texas proceedings. Attorney Winston expressed serious concerns about Sophia's safety and Lauryn's instability. The next day, the Georgia courts had exercised jurisdiction of the case according to the Uniform Child Custody Jurisdiction and Enforcement Act (UCCJEA).

I now had retained two attorneys, one in Atlanta and another in Dallas. I was in constant contact with Attorney Winston in Georgia. She and Judge Dempsey were doing their best to keep the jurisdiction in Georgia.

The Dallas court date was reset to July 18. Attorney Lester filed a motion to change custody. Previously, she had filed a motion for access to visitation. The motion stated that we had made multiple attempts to get visitation with Sophia. Lauryn had continually violated Judge Dempsey's orders. The motion stated in part:

> The Court should order that the Defendant and the child be ordered to submit to a psychological evaluation. The current Guardian Ad Litem in this case addressed issues of custody, mental health of the child, education needs and access to appropriate medical and educational instruction and alienation of affection related to

the minor child, as it is a growing concern that the mother is causing serious harm to the child.

Lauryn and Attorney Nimpson were working vigorously to transfer jurisdiction of the case back to the Dallas Courts. I had secured a Dallas attorney to represent me for the July 18 hearing. Attorney Cantos had been a law enforcement officer many years in Dallas. He was a powerful and aggressive attorney. I referred to him as the "bulldog."

Lauryn had not followed through on the judge's temporary orders. She had not taken Sophia to be assessed as the judge had ordered. She had not allowed me to have supervised visits.

During the July 18 hearing, the presiding judge ordered that I have unsupervised visits with Sophia from July 21 through August 4, 2012. We were to have the exchange at the police department in Humble, Texas, near Houston. The judge then transferred the case to Harris County. We had won a temporary victory.

We were finally out of the Dallas courts, at least temporarily. Lauryn was visibly upset about the judge's order. I knew that she would fight this with all her power.

While in court, I had coordinated with a process server to have Lauryn officially notified of our intent to file for custody in Fulton County, Georgia. Lauryn was attempting to move jurisdiction to Texas, and I was fighting to keep jurisdiction in Georgia.

After we had won this small victory, I wrote a letter to the State Bar of Texas' Office of the Chief of Disciplinary Counsel. I filed an ethics complaint against Attorney Nimpson.

His license to practice law in Texas had already been temporarily suspended. My primary concern was that he had knowingly and willfully helped Lauryn to file false statements. The Texas Bar Association refused to take any further actions against him.

The day finally arrived for me to pick up Sophia in Humble, Texas. Crystal wanted to make the long trip with me, but I never wanted her to be involved when Lauryn was present due to safety concerns. Lauryn did not want Crystal around Sophia. I decided to take the trip alone. I was nervous the entire trip. I finally arrived in Humble, Texas, at 4:30 p.m. The exchange was to occur at 6:00 p.m.

I nervously waited outside the police station. I was praying out loud, hoping that the trip would not be in vain this time. I had been to Houston just a few weeks earlier, and Lauryn hadn't shown up. I saw a black vehicle pull up at 6:30p.m. that evening. Lauryn slowly emerged from the vehicle with Sophia behind her. I saw a look of fear in Sophia's eyes. I could tell that Sophia was terrified of her mom. Lauryn controlled her every move. She was compliant or she would be beaten. I was surprised to see a man and a woman also appear with Lauryn.

We met inside the police station. I went to the front desk to let them know that we were there for an exchange. I showed them the court orders from Dallas. I could see Lauryn outside the glass doors talking to Sophia. I watched as Sophia cried profusely. I knew that Sophia would play along with Lauryn's wishes and demands. She had learned to manage Lauryn's emotions. I had learned that children of parents with borderline personality disorder often had to manage their parents' emotions. It was a way of staying safe.

After several minutes of waiting, Lauryn came inside with Sophia. Sophia was crying and told Lauryn that she did not want to leave with me.

I kept hearing the woman who was with Lauryn say to Sophia, "Baby, you need to go with your dad. He loves you. He has been fighting for you for eleven years. He wouldn't have come this far to harm you. Just get in the car and go with him. I will be there for you. You can call me at any time."

After hearing this, Lauryn told Sophia, "You need to go with him, pumpkin."

I picked up Sophia's bags and walked toward my SUV. I put her bags inside. For several minutes, Lauryn kissed on her and told her that she would stay in close contact with her by phone. I opened the door as Sophia got in the back seat. As Lauryn turned her back, the woman who was with Lauryn dropped her business card on the ground next to me. I picked it up and put it in my pocket.

I slowly backed out of the parking lot and drove back to Dallas. I breathed a deep sigh of relief. I could not believe that she was finally in the car with me. I could not wait to get home to call the woman who had left me her business card.

Her name was Linda Forbes. I had met her many years ago at Sophia's birthday party in Houston. I believed that things were finally beginning to turn around.

Turning Around

Sophia was finally with me. I had fought a long and arduous battle, but it was all worth it. She was almost eleven years old. Lauryn had prevented me from having a relationship with Sophia since the day she was born. Lauryn wanted Sophia all to herself.

I enjoyed the long drive back to Dallas. Sophia listened to her favorite music the entire trip back home. She liked different genres of music. She turned the radio from hip-hop, to R&B, rock and country. I was amazed at how many things we had in common. I began to realize that I had missed out on some of the most important milestones in her life. I was angry that Lauryn had selfishly done this to punish me. She had done harm to Sophia in the process.

During the four-hour drive to Dallas, Lauryn called Sophia at least eight times. I didn't block her calls to Sophia as she had done to me. Sophia would always answer as she had been told. I could tell that she was trying to control Sophia. I did nothing to interfere with the calls from her mom. I had tried to make calls to Sophia over the past ten years and had been unable to do so. Yet, Lauryn monopolized her time.

I arrived home late that night. Megan and Moriah were waiting for us to arrive. They all hugged Sophia and helped to get her luggage out of the car. There was an immediate bond between the girls, especially between Megan and Sophia. They were closer in age to one another. We stayed up late into the night talking. Sophia had longed to have friends and big sisters. She vaguely remembered spending time with them when she was much younger.

I called Linda Forbes as soon as I arrived back in Dallas. She was eager to talk with me. She told me that she had attempted to give me her contact information during Sophia's birthday party in Houston.

Lauryn made sure that we were not able to communicate with one another. Lauryn had to own and possess every relationship that she had with others. Everybody in her life had to respond to her on her terms, or she would terminate the relationship.

Linda and I talked for hours about Lauryn's treatment of Sophia. She shared many stories about how Lauryn had left Sophia at home for hours and even a couple of days at a time. Sophia would be alone in their apartment, afraid to contact anyone except Linda.

For many years, she had managed to keep Sophia from telling the authorities. She did tell Linda some of the bad things that had happened to her. She would ask Linda questions, like, "Is this right?" Linda and her husband, Kevin, would always listen to Sophia and be there for her. They were Sophia's guardian angels. Sophia at least had two safe adults whom she could rely upon.

Linda shared with me several stories about Lauryn's abusive behavior toward Sophia. One night in particular, Lauryn had spent the weekend with Brian. Sophia had awakened to an empty apartment. She panicked. She immediately called Linda and asked her what she should do. Linda said that she would stay on the phone with her, and then she would call Lauryn. Linda told Lauryn that Sophia could have been placed in danger by being at home alone at such a young age. Linda threatened to call the authorities if Lauryn didn't return home to care for Sophia. Linda had to be careful in sharing her thoughts with Lauryn. She would cut off anyone who challenged her.

Sophia would often go hungry. Lauryn would leave her with cereal and milk and a few microwavable foods. Once they were gone, she had to wait for Lauryn to return home before she could eat. Lauryn would go ballistic if Sophia called her while she was gone. Sophia only had Linda and Kevin to rely on for support.

On Sunday morning, I told Sophia to get ready for church. She refused to go to church, so I decided to stay home. I believe that Lauryn had told Sophia to be defiant and not to go along with my wishes. It was a method of control for Lauryn.

Lauryn felt as if she would lose control of Sophia if she bonded with me. I told Sophia that we would be going to church the rest of the time that she stayed with us. Our church had prayed for her and helped me in any way that they could. I had always believed that God had made provisions for us to get Sophia. Our family was incomplete without her.

We went to ride bumper cars that evening. During our time together at dinner, Sophia told me several times, "Please just drop the case, Gerald." I told her that I was simply trying to build a relationship with her. I was not trying to take her from her mother. Lauryn continued to call her, even during dinner. I knew that it was Lauryn who was putting her up to asking me to drop the case.

I decided to take off work the following week. I wanted to bond with Sophia. I knew that Sophia and I had a lot of catching up to do. I wanted her to have a positive experience and to adjust well. I woke up early Monday morning to check on Sophia. She was asleep when I first checked on her. I checked on her every hour or so.

Around twelve-thirty in the afternoon, I went into Sophia's room. She was sitting on the bed rubbing her fingers. I asked her what was wrong. She then blurted out, "I burned my fingers."

I asked her how. She said, "I burned them on the stove in the kitchen." She had spread some Neosporin on both of her thumbs.

"Are you okay?" I asked.

She said, "Yes, I am okay."

"Does it hurt?"

"No, it doesn't hurt."

I held her hands and took a closer look. I did not see any signs of redness. I began to wonder if Lauryn had put her up to this. She had already reported me to the Texas Department of Family and Protective Services many years ago. I knew that Lauryn would go to any extreme to prevent me from seeing Sophia. I told Sophia that I would have to take her to the doctor or an emergency room to make sure that everything was all right. Sophia said that she was okay and didn't need to see a doctor.

I then asked for her to go with me to the kitchen. I touched the burners on the stove. None of them had been used that morning or early afternoon. I asked Sophia who had turned on the stove. She said that she did not know who had turned it on. I was confident that Lauryn had set up the entire plot.

I told Sophia once again that I was taking her to get some treatment for the burn on her hand. She said that she had just sent pictures to her mom. Lauryn had told her not to go to the doctor with me. I made a firm decision at that point that I would at least take her to a pharmacy to look at her finger. I told her to take a shower and get dressed.

I took Sophia with me to the pharmacist at Walgreens. The pharmacist looked at her fingers and said that she did not see any burn marks. I knew that the entire story had been concocted by Lauryn to use against me in court. I documented everything, including the visit to the pharmacist.

Lauryn was an expert at manipulation. She was losing in both Georgia and in Texas. She needed to do something to turn the tide. Lauryn continued to call Sophia at least every hour. This time, she started to call Sophia on an app so that she could see Sophia. Most importantly, Lauryn was trying to see what was going on in our house. Lauryn wanted Sophia to record her every move in our home.

This could be dangerous. I didn't know if Lauryn would use the information to break into our house. I told Sophia that she could not use the video to talk with Lauryn.

I e-mailed Lauryn that evening and told her what had happened with Sophia's fingers. I also told her that Sophia had a cough and runny nose that wouldn't go away.

Lauryn had never allowed me to know Sophia's physician. I literally knew nothing about Sophia's health. Sophia had seemed to have a constant cold since she was a child. I had begun to believe that she was so stressed and traumatized by her mother that her immune system might have been compromised.

The rest of the week was uneventful. I took Sophia to East Texas to visit her aunts, uncles, and cousins. They had heard about the horrible things that Lauryn had done so many years to keep Sophia away from me. They couldn't believe that she was finally with me after ten long years!

I was saddened that my sister, Maria, had passed away without ever having a chance to see Sophia, except when she was a newborn. I was angry that Lauryn didn't care that so many of Sophia's aunts and uncles didn't get the chance to see her grow up.

Things had been calm for the past few days. Lauryn continued to call, but at least there were no more extreme incidents. On Monday afternoon, the local police department knocked on our door. The police said that they were there to do a welfare check. They said that Lauryn had called and told them to check on Sophia and to make sure that she was okay. Lauryn had sent several e-mails stating that she had not been able to speak with Sophia that morning.

I asked Sophia when she had last spoken with Lauryn. She said, "last night."

I had spent many years not getting to speak with or see Sophia. Lauryn had missed a few hours speaking with her and was calling the police. She demanded total obedience and obeisance from Sophia and everyone around her.

During Sophia's last night with us, we went to eat and listen to music at the Caribbean Grille. It was a great place to eat Jamaican food. Sophia enjoyed the food and live reggae music. During one of the songs, Sophia asked if she could go up on stage. The lead singer gave her the microphone, and she began to sing with the band. She seemed such a natural. She seemed free.

Do No Harm

I felt more strongly than ever that I had to get Sophia away from Lauryn. The Georgia courts were doing their best to help. A thirty-day status conference was scheduled on August 7, 2012. Judge Dempsey was very concerned about the false reports. She was alarmed that Lauryn had encouraged Sophia to stage her fingers being burned. By this time, my attorney had filed a motion for modification of custody. I felt good about the odds.

We were concerned that Lauryn was not responding to any of the communication from the court about the thirty-day status hearings. Lauryn would later allege that she had not been informed of the hearings. The State of Georgia allowed persons to be notified of court hearings via e-mail. Lauryn had consented to the process. Now she was claiming that she had not been notified.

I made multiple attempts to communicate with Sophia after I returned her to Lauryn in late July. Once again, Lauryn did not allow her to accept my calls. Linda Forbes was communicating with Lauryn and me at the same time. Linda would have been in danger had Lauryn found out.

Linda Forbes had informed me that Lauryn had planned to leave Sophia in Spring, Texas with her grandfather while she moved back to her job in Atlanta. Lauryn had taken off some time from her teaching job. She was still fighting to keep the case in Texas even while she continued to reside in Alpharetta, Georgia.

I was concerned about Sophia staying with her grandfather. He drank alcohol heavily. He also had a lot of mental problems. He had spent many of his earlier years in and out of jail. He loved to tell war stories about his escapades. He was in his sixties but acted like he was in his twenties.

He could not provide the support and guidance that Sophia so desperately needed. She had endured enough damage with Lauryn. Now she was going to be living with a grandfather who was incapable of caring for her.

Sophia loved her grandfather. She had spent a lot of time with him when she was a child. Even though he and Lauryn had a rocky relationship, he gave Sophia a lot of attention.

Sophia's uncle, "Big Mo," also lived with Sophia's grandfather. Big Mo suffered from schizophrenia. He would often hear voices. He paced the floor a lot and talked to himself most of the time. Sophia talked about him a lot.

I was pleased that Linda lived close by. She would help to provide stability, nurturing, guidance, and support that Big Mo and her grandfather could not provide.

Lauryn had not allowed Sophia to develop friendships with other children her age. Linda Forbes' son, Carter, was close to Sophia. Lauryn didn't feel threatened by him.

While I knew where Sophia was living and attending school, I didn't want to cause any further disruption for her. The case was still moving forward in Georgia.

Our next status hearing was held with Judge Dempsey, Attorney Lester, and Attorney Winston on September 12. The specifics of the merger of the custody case and the visitation case were discussed. Judge Dempsey was supportive of moving forward with custody. She wanted to ensure that Lauryn had been informed of the proceedings. She was also concerned that the Texas case was pending with Judge Alvarez in Dallas County.

A few weeks later, we received news from Judge Alvarez that the court had failed to prosecute the case for want of prosecution. Both judges in Dallas had dismissed the two motions that had been filed. We celebrated the news from the courts. Lauryn had done her dead-level best to get jurisdiction moved from Georgia to Texas based on false allegations. The courts didn't fall for it. It was an early Christmas gift.

I visited with Sophia several times at her school in Spring, Texas. Her grades were beginning to drop. Lauryn had done Sophia's homework for many years. Her constant criticism of Sophia had taken a toll. She didn't feel confident about her ability to do the schoolwork. Lauryn had often called her a "dumb b****" Sophia didn't have any supervision or structure while living with her grandfather. He was busy drinking and chasing women. Linda visited Sophia on a daily basis and ensured that her daily needs were met. During one of her visits, she found several wine bottles underneath Sophia's bed. She was fearful that Sophia had begun to drink to deal with her problems.

Children with toxic stress and maltreatment often resort to drugs or alcohol to cope with their pain and trauma. I was fearful that Sophia would become addicted to alcohol or drugs. Linda and I confronted her about the wine bottles found underneath her bed. She acknowledged that she had drunk some of the alcohol that her grandfather had left in the apartment.

Linda continued to visit Sophia daily. Lauryn didn't provide any type of support for Sophia. She was busy trying to keep her relationship with Brian Benson. Sophia was not her priority.

I had planned for Sophia to spend Thanksgiving with us for the first time. I didn't think that Lauryn would consent to the visit. With Linda's help, Lauryn agreed for Sophia to spend a few days with us for Thanksgiving. It would be my first-time having Sophia with us for a major holiday. Sophia spent three days with us. The visit went well.

Lauryn continued to call her, but I could tell that the distance from Lauryn was allowing her to mature. She was beginning to develop her own identity. Sophia bonded well with Megan and Moriah. I felt that our family was finally coming together.

Another status hearing occurred on November 29. We discussed the specifics of the final custody orders. Judge Dempsey and Attorney Winston expressed concern about Sophia's and my family's safety. I told them that I wanted to move forward. I was confident that we would be safe.

For the next several weeks, I worked with my attorney on the final order. The Final Order on Modification, Custody and Support was signed on December 17, 2012. We did our best to include provisions that would ensure that the case would not be overturned. We knew that Lauryn would not accept the conditions of the order unless it was enforceable by law. Judge Dempsey and Attorney Winston stated the following in the final order:

> The defendant systematically sought to alienate the affections of the parties' daughter and refused to obey court orders requiring the defendant to allow Plaintiff to exercise visitation with child on multiple occasions. A 60-day status conference was held on March 16, 2012. The Defendant was ordered to not remove the minor child from the jurisdiction of the Court or to travel outside the State without a Court Order or written agreement signed by both parties. Defendant failed to appear. Defendant did, however, remove the minor child from the state of Georgia without notice of the Court, without permission of the Court and in violation of the order of the Court. The Defendant went to such great lengths in preventing Plaintiff from visiting the parties' minor child that Plaintiff hired private investigators to determine the whereabouts of his daughter. Defendant's repeated moves with the minor child resulted in the minor child having to make multiple moves and attend several different schools after the entry of the 2006 order.
>
> The Court finds that Georgia is the home state of the minor child and that the Defendant moved with the minor child to Texas, in violation of this Court's Temporary Order, in an effort to avoid the jurisdiction of the Court and to engage in forum shopping. The Court finds that during a March 16 hearing, the Defendant mother lied to the Court concerning the whereabouts of the minor child stating that the child was in

Michigan when in fact the child was in Georgia, a fact she later admitted to the Court. The Court finds that the Defendant filed a restraining order against the Plaintiff in Texas for the sole purpose of obstructing Plaintiff's visitation with the minor child. The Court finds that the Defendant actively sought to alienate the affections of the parties' daughter toward Plaintiff father.

Plaintiff father is hereby awarded primary physical custody of the minor child. The mother, until further order of this Court or by written recommendation by the child's psychologist or psychiatrist or licensed professional counselor acting under the supervision of this Court, shall not have regular court-ordered visitation with the minor child. Due to the risks of the mother fleeing with the child, as well as her ongoing alienation, control and influence over the child, the mother shall have only supervised visitation with the child at this time.

The Harris County Texas Sheriff's Office shall assist in the pick-up of the minor child and shall ensure that the transfer is accomplished in a peaceful manner. Transfer of custody shall occur at the end of the school day on December 20, 2012. Mother does not have to be present at the time of the pick-up to avoid any disruption at the school or other location child may be found.

The final order was signed by Judge Dempsey. I was ecstatic! It had taken a little over a year. I had gone to Georgia in hopes of getting visitation, and I had been awarded primary custody. The systems that had worked against my daughter and me now seemed to work in our favor. Victory seemed closer than ever before.

Keep the Faith

My family and I celebrated the victory. Our church celebrated as well. We knew that this was not the end of the story. I called Linda Forbes and shared the news with her. She and her family had supported Sophia for many years, even at the risk of their personal safety. They deserved a lot of credit for the victory. I thanked her for the many years that she had been a guardian angel for Sophia. I told her the date of the pickup order. I knew that Lauryn would retaliate once she knew that the Georgia courts had awarded me primary custody of Sophia. I thought about her plans to run with Sophia out of the country.

A few days later, I traveled to Houston to find an attorney that would help me to get a pickup order from a Harris County court. I found a great attorney in Attorney Hardy. She was a young attorney who cared deeply about children. She advised me that Texas might not accept the pickup order from Georgia. Texas courts don't like to accept out-of-state orders unless they are issued by a Texas court.

After much deliberation, I attempted to pick Sophia up at Twin Creeks Middle School in Spring, Texas, on December 20 as the Georgia courts had ordered. I had consulted with the Harris County Sheriff's Department prior to my visit.

I met with the school principal and gave him a certified copy of the Georgia orders, including the pickup order. The principal consulted with the sheriff's deputies. They informed me that I needed to get a Texas court order for the Georgia order to be enforced in Texas. It was another temporary setback. I had endured many setbacks. I didn't lose faith. I had hoped that Sophia would spend Christmas with us. I remained hopeful. We were too close to give up now.

I shared the news with Attorney Hardy. She told me that she would begin the process of getting an order issued from Harris County to enforce the Georgia order. I purchased Sophia Christmas gifts and mailed them to her. Our family celebrated Christmas without her. We were hopeful that Sophia would join us soon.

I called Sophia on Christmas Day. I could tell that she was disappointed that she didn't get to spend Christmas with us. Sophia said that she had received a laptop from me with all the bells and whistles. Lauryn had bought her a flip phone to replace her iPhone that Lauryn had broken in a fit of anger. Brian had spent Christmas with Lauryn and Sophia in Houston. Lauryn had bought Brian suits, ties, and belts. Lauryn had always put the man that she was dating before Sophia. Lauryn told Sophia that she was keeping the laptop for herself.

I was confident that Sophia would be with us in a matter of weeks. I was at least speaking with Sophia every evening. Lauryn was back in Atlanta taking care of Brian. I continued to visit Sophia at her school.

Attorney Hardy continued to work with the Harris County courts to get a writ of attachment. This would satisfy the Harris County Sheriff to enforce the order and for the school to permit me to pick her up. The document was filed on March 1 in the Harris County courts.

I had coordinated with Attorney Hardy to arrange on the date of Monday, March 4 to pick up Sophia at Twin Creeks Middle School. The court had approved the writ of attachment. We had coordinated everything with the Harris County Sheriff's Department. I had arrived the night before. I had never been so nervous. The last pickup effort had not gone well. I didn't know if Lauryn would sabotage things. I knew that Linda Forbes would keep everything confidential.

Early Monday morning, I arrived at Sophia's school. Several Harris County sheriffs accompanied me. There were five or six deputies on hand just in case things went wrong. The deputies escorted me into the school. The school administrators, parents, and students were gazing at us. I presented the writ of attachment from the Harris County, Texas courts and the pickup order from Georgia. The principal escorted me into his office. The principal called in the school counselor. The school counselor and an assistant principal went to get Sophia and brought her to the office.

Once Sophia arrived, she was surprised to see me back at her school, this time with a coterie of law enforcement officers. I could tell that she was nervous.

I told Sophia, "I am here to get you and take you back with me. These officers are here to make sure that you are safe."

Sophia said with a nervous grin, "Can I call my mom?"

I said, "Yes."

I gave the principal Lauryn's mobile phone number. He called her, and she immediately answered.

"What is wrong with my daughter?" Lauryn said.

The principal shared with her that I had an order from the Harris County courts to pick Sophia up from school.

Lauryn started to scream and yell, "He cannot pick up my daughter. He has molested her. Please, sir, don't let him take her, please."

The principal continued to talk with Lauryn in a calm voice. She continued to scream. One of the sheriff's deputies then began to talk with Lauryn.

"Lauryn, we are here to enforce the writ of attachment that has been issued by a Harris County judge for Gerald Ingram to pick up his daughter." They talked a few minutes longer.

Lauryn screamed, "I will be on a plane to get my daughter today," and hung up the phone.

I knew that Lauryn meant business. Lauryn could never take defeat in anything. Lauryn was teaching class at North Atlanta High School when she received the call at 10:30 a.m. She immediately left her class and ran to the principal's office. She told them that it was an emergency.

"My daughter has been kidnapped!" she said.

Lauryn didn't take the time to get any of her possessions. She immediately called Brian Benson. He and Matthew Nimpson always bailed her out of trouble when needed. She told Brian that I had kidnapped Sophia from school and that she needed to take a trip to

Houston that afternoon. She told Brian to meet her at the airport. Brian was teaching school too. He met Lauryn at the airport and purchased her a one-way ticket to Houston. He gave her money to get a rental car. Lauryn was on the ground in Houston by 4:00 p.m. that same day. She immediately got a rental car and told Attorney Nimpson to start working on a way for her to get Sophia back. He told her that he would help her in any way that he could.

Lauryn first stopped to visit with her father at her apartment. He always went along with her plans. He felt that he owed that to her, since he was not there for her during much of her childhood. Lauryn had allowed him to live a lifestyle that he hadn't been able to afford. He enjoyed staying at a new apartment that Lauryn had leased for him and Sophia.

The Attorney General's Office of Texas had stopped the child support payments that Lauryn had been receiving. She was livid. She couldn't afford to keep the apartment near Houston. Brian was helping to take care of her while she was in Atlanta.

Lauryn had also called Linda Forbes while she was driving to Dallas. She told her that I had kidnapped Sophia. Lauryn didn't know that Linda had helped with the planning. Linda couldn't share her real thoughts. She was trying to keep a line of communication open with Lauryn while also trying to protect Sophia and keep me informed of Lauryn's every move. It was a tough juggling act.

Lauryn drove to meet Attorney Nimpson that evening. She stayed up all night and planned a strategy to get Sophia back. She had told Linda that all that she needed to do to get Attorney Nimpson's help was to give him some good sex and he would sign off on anything.

Sophia and I spent all day Monday on the drive back to Dallas. We planned on where she would attend school. She was excited to rejoin the family. Megan and Moriah were excited to see Sophia as well. They also knew that Lauryn was a real threat to their safety. They had grown up hearing about the horrible things that she had done. Sophia had informed us that Lauryn always kept a gun that her grandfather had given her.

"She will shoot up the house," Sophia said.

Sophia told us a story about Lauryn receiving a knock on the door when they lived in Alpharetta, Georgia. Lauryn had stood behind the front door with her gun drawn. Sophia had seen her with a gun on many occasions. She knew that her mother would use it.

Sophia also told us that Lauryn had laughingly told her that she had thought about doing a drive-by on our house. She said that she could imagine Crystal and the girls screaming as they were being shot. Lauryn loved to share stories about violence with Sophia. Sophia had witnessed Lauryn's violent streak on many occasions.

I allowed Sophia to stay home from school the next day. We had both been through a lot. We went to play games and eat at Dave & Buster's that evening in Arlington. On Wednesday, I took Sophia to get registered for school. She was excited about attending a new school and meeting new friends. Sophia had attended over eight different schools by the seventh grade. I was glad that we would finally get her into a stable and consistent home and school environment. I had a team of doctors and therapists to support Sophia.

Crystal picked Sophia up from school. We knew that Lauryn was busy plotting how to get Sophia back from us. We sat and had dinner and talked about her first day at her new school. Suddenly, we heard a loud knock on the front door. I answered the door.

A deputy sheriff asked, "Is Sophia here?"

I said, "Yes."

He then asked for her to please come to the door. Sophia came to the door, and two officers reached out to her and told her that she must leave with them. At that moment, he gave me a legal document stating that I must appear in court on March 19, 2013 at 1:30 p.m. A hearing would be held to determine the "possession of the child."

I couldn't believe what I was hearing. I could not imagine what Lauryn had done to get the courts to remove Sophia from us. I had won primary custody in Georgia and had a court in Harris County to issue a writ of attachment. I was beside myself.

The next day, I immediately contacted Attorney Hardy. She began work on getting a new writ of attachment to be issued in Harris County. I also contacted Attorney Cantos, who had helped to get the cases in Dallas dismissed in the summer of 2012. I met with him at his office the next day. We developed a strategy to respond to Lauryn's allegations. Lauryn had written the following affidavit:

> On March 3, 2013, Sophia made an outcry statement wherein she stated that in the summer of 2012 after a long nap on the couch she awoke and was looking for her stepsisters. Respondent heard Sophia walking around looking for her stepsisters and called her into his office. Respondent was in his office wearing boxer shorts and a t-shirt when he began hitting his leg to signal for Sophia to come over and sit on his lap. Reluctantly, Sophia went over and sat on his lap and asked where Crystal and her daughters were. Respondent stated that they were at the mall. Respondent then began rubbing Sophia. Sophia immediately jumped up and jumped off his lap in tears. Respondent began telling Sophia that he was sorry and not to tell anyone. Respondent told Sophia that he would lose his job if she told anyone and all the people who work for him would lose their jobs too and that if they lost their jobs: "Somebody might kill your mother; you don't want that, right?" He also told her that her stepsisters would hate her and that something may happen to her mom. Sophia went on to tell him, "I don't trust you anymore," that she did not want to be hurt by him and that he needed help. Upon discovery of the incident. I advised Sophia that I would make a report. She stated that she did not want to make a report because she was scared something would happen to me and she did not want Respondent to go to jail. Less than 24 hours later and before I could get back to Texas my child was kidnapped by Respondent from Twin Creeks Middle School located in Spring, Texas.

> She is now in danger of future sexual advances and assaults by Respondent. Based on these facts, the Petitioner believes that the Respondent's continued possession of the child will create and is creating a serious, immediate threat to the child's physical and emotional well-being. Respondent will remove the child from the jurisdiction of this Court unless the child is immediately removed from Respondent's possession.

I could not fathom that Lauryn would stoop to this level. My sister, Belinda, had told me years earlier that Lauryn would make such an allegation against me. I was angry and beside myself. Would the court believe this lie? I had already had a bad experience with the child welfare system in Texas. Would they arrest me and ask questions later? Fortunately, they didn't arrest me while they conducted the investigation.

I was running out of patience and money. I had hired four attorneys in two different states over the past eighteen months. I had to pay the fees for the guardian ad litem. I had hired several private investigators.

I was traveling heavily for my job. I called my immediate supervisor to discuss the situation. He told me to take as much time as needed to deal with the situation. He knew that the allegations made against me were false. The drama had been unfolding since 1999. It was now 2013. It had been fourteen years of manipulation and attacks. Sophia had been beaten by Lauryn in the womb before she was even born.

Thankfully, my church was supportive of me. Crystal and her family were also very supportive. My sisters continued to support me as well. Attorney Hardy was working on a Harris County writ of habeas corpus while Attorney Cantos was preparing for the March 19 hearing in Dallas. The date of the hearing finally arrived. Matthew Nimpson and I were on the same elevator as we were going to court. Crystal was standing by my side. I was losing patience. Lauryn would not have been able to file all the false legal documents without his help. He had young children of his own. I began to wonder if he had a soul.

Attorney Cantos and I sat in court waiting for the hearing to begin. Lauryn had not yet appeared. Judge Gonzales asked both parties to approach the bench. Attorney Nimpson noted that Lauryn would not be able to attend the hearing due to her employment as a teacher in Atlanta. The court proceeded without her presence.

Attorney Nimpson attempted to question the legitimacy of Georgia's final court awarding me primary custody of Sophia. He presented to the judge the concerns about Sophia's alleged sexual abuse. Judge Gonzales listened intently. Attorney Cantos presented a strong case. His first argument was about legal jurisdiction and prior rulings in the case. He referenced the prior judge's dismissal of the case in the summer of 2012. The hearing lasted less than an hour.

After hearing testimony that the Texas Department of Family and Protective Services and the Cedar Hill Police Department were conducting investigations about the alleged sexual abuse, Judge Gonzales dismissed the case.

Attorney Nimpson had filed a motion to modify custody a few days later. The judge denied the request for modification. I immediately called Attorney Hardy and informed her that Judge Gonzales had dismissed the writ of attachment issued in Dallas County. She had worked with Harris County courts to get a hearing set for March 23. Lauryn's attempt to say that I had "kidnapped" Sophia hadn't worked.

I had also begun speaking with a detective about Lauryn's allegations. Her name was Detective Karney. Lauryn had initially filed the sexual abuse allegations in Houston. Since I lived in Dallas County, a local detective was leading the investigation. She called me initially to ask a few questions about my history with Lauryn. I spoke with her about the recent court cases in both Georgia and Texas. I also shared with her copies of several legal documents. I wanted her to know the full story.

Detective Karney said, "Somebody is going to jail over this. I don't know if it is you or Lauryn, but somebody is going to jail."

I felt a great deal of comfort with her statement. I knew that I had not done what Lauryn had alleged. I was confident that things would work in our favor.

I had spoken to more than six different detectives since I had met Lauryn. None of them had resulted in convictions. I had hoped that she would be able to see through Lauryn's lies.

Lauryn had allowed Sophia to spend a few days with Linda Forbes. Sophia told Linda that Lauryn had forced her to make up the story about the abuse.

Lauryn told Sophia, "You don't want Mommy to go to jail, do you?"

Lauryn had rehearsed the story for several days with Sophia. She showed her how to answer questions and to cry if necessary. While Sophia was being questioned in Houston, Lauryn was giving her signals on how to respond. She told Sophia to tell the police that I abused drugs and that Crystal was physically abusive toward her. Sophia went along with the story.

That night, Sophia broke down and told Linda that it was all made up. Linda comforted Sophia. The next day, she encouraged Sophia to go with her to Dallas County to tell the truth to Detective Karney. Initially, Sophia was skeptical. She knew that there would be hell to pay if Lauryn ever found out that Sophia was "disloyal" to her.

Linda called Detective Karney to tell her that she was bringing Sophia to her office for an interview. Linda shared Sophia's statement that Lauryn had forced her to make false statements. Detective Karney interviewed Sophia separately. After the interviews, I was contacted by Detective Karney. She told me that she was confident that Lauryn forced Sophia to make false statements. A warrant would be issued for her arrest.

In the meantime, Attorney Hardy was working on yet another writ of attachment in order for me to pick Sophia in Houston. We planned to have Linda transport Sophia to the local sheriff's department. I felt much more comfortable now that we were meeting at a law enforcement office. That morning, Linda, Attorney Hardy, the deputies, and I met at the sheriff's department. We exchanged legal documents. A few minutes later, I was headed back to Dallas with my Sophia, hopefully for the last time.

Now that Sophia was back with us, we were jubilant. The Cedar Hill Police Department had been incredibly supportive during this time. They knew that Lauryn was unstable and dangerous. I had enough documentation to demonstrate that she was a threat to Sophia, our family, and public safety. Things were beginning to turn around.

Amber Alert

Sophia was adjusting well to living with us. She finally felt a sense of freedom. She could play with other kids her age. She was attending school and beginning to develop friends. I was taking her to therapy at least once a week. I had a team of professionals who supported Sophia, including a psychiatrist and a therapist who specialized in trauma. I knew a lot about wraparound planning through my many years working with youth and their families. Sophia needed a lot of care and support to make the adjustment after living with Lauryn for twelve years.

The adjustment to living with us was not without its challenges. She had become accustomed to a lot of drama. Although we had challenges, they were not as severe as those that she had experienced with Lauryn.

My primary concern was about our safety. I knew that Lauryn would be arrested at some point for filing false police reports. It was only a matter of time. I also knew that Lauryn would retaliate against us. We had installed a security system at our home as a safety measure. We knew that Lauryn would be lurking in our community.

A few days later, I received a call from Sophia's school. Lauryn had attempted to check her out of school in violation of the court's orders. She had met with the school principal and became hostile. Lauryn began to threaten and cuss at the principal. The school police became involved. When the police ran a background check, they found out that a warrant had been issued for Lauryn's arrest for filing false police reports. Lauryn was arrested on-site. She was transported to the Dallas County jail.

Detective Karney had kept her word and issued a warrant for Lauryn's arrest for filing false police reports. Attorney Nimpson had her bonded out the next day. Lauryn was enraged. How could she be arrested? For what? She thought that she was impervious to any consequences for her behavior. I knew that Lauryn would retaliate for the arrest. Sophia kept telling us that Lauryn was going to do something crazy.

"She will shoot up the house," Sophia kept reminding us.

After the arrest, the Cedar Hill Police Department transported Sophia to school for a few weeks. They also placed a police car as a decoy in front of our house for several days. Everybody was on high alert. A few days later, Lauryn would do the unimaginable. The day of infamy came when Sophia had returned home from school. We had rehearsed plans in case Lauryn ever attempted to kidnap Sophia. Our plan was for Crystal and Sophia not to resist and to contact the police as soon as possible. If they resisted, I felt that they could be harmed.

While Sophia was home from school, Lauryn began to call her on her cell phone. She told Sophia that her grandfather wanted to see her. Sophia kept telling her that she could not leave the house. Crystal and my niece Brandy had left to go to the store. Lauryn wanted to know the whereabouts of Crystal and me so that she could make her move. On their way back home, Crystal and Brandy saw a person a few hundred feet from our house.

Crystal screamed, "Oh, my god. That's Lauryn."

She was parked down the street from our house so that her vehicle couldn't be detected.

Crystal quickly drove home to check on Sophia. Brandy was a former law enforcement officer. She and Crystal quickly went into the house to check on Sophia. As they entered, Sophia was on the phone talking with Lauryn.

Within a few minutes, Lauryn was in front of our house on the phone, talking with Sophia!

"I am going to take you to see your grandfather, Sophia. He and your mommy are sick, pumpkin. You don't want us sick, do you? Just give Mommy a hug and kiss. They won't let me see you. Your granddad is here…"

Sophia was still on her cell phone talking to her mom when she walked into the front yard.

Lauryn rolled down her window and said, "Come here, baby. Come here, baby… Come here."

Lauryn had promised Sophia that her grandfather was in the car with her. It was all a lie to get Sophia in the car! Sophia walked over to the window as Lauryn grabbed her arm and pulled her into the car. Lauryn quickly sped off.

Crystal called Sophia's cell phone numerous times. She finally answered.

Crystal said, "Are you okay, Sophia?"

Lauryn grabbed the phone and said, "Yes b****, she's okay… She's with her mom."

Crystal started to follow her down the street while calling the Cedar Hill Police Department.

It appeared that during the phone call, Lauryn started to read Sophia a letter that she alleged that I wrote. The letter in part said:

> Thank God we got Sophia because she landed in our trap right where we wanted her to be. We don't want her in our f****** house. If she portrayed you like that, what do you think she would do to our family? We are gonna send that b**** out of the house as quick as possible. That b**** wants to be a rapper; she is dumb as f***. My real daughters don't even think of her as their sister. They want her out of the house. Yeah, my pockets are a little bit heavier now that you are sending child support! I told you that you should have gotten an abortion, but your dumb ass wouldn't do it! Me and Crystal are laughing so loud now!

Lauryn was at it again. She always wrote letters and claimed that I had written them. This time, she wanted to convince Sophia that we didn't want her in our house. We were the enemy.

Crystal called me on my cell phone. I was only a few miles away from home. I quickly drove home. Crystal and Brandy were on the phone with the Cedar Hill Police Department. They had been very responsive. They had arrested Lauryn a few days earlier at Sophia's school. The race was on to find Sophia!

For the next several hours, the Cedar Hill Police Department called Lauryn and pleaded with her to return Sophia. Lauryn kept saying that she had the legal right to take Sophia with her. Lauryn would not share with the police her location. The police were somehow able to track her location on 75 North headed towards the Oklahoma border.

The police were also able to contact Lauryn's attorney and boyfriend, Attorney Nimpson. I was confident that he knew Lauryn's whereabouts and plans. The police were able to get Attorney Nimpson on a three-way call with Lauryn. Lauryn refused to share any information.

After her conversation with Matthew and the police, Lauryn refused to answer her phone again. She had purchased a TracFone at a local Wal-Mart. Lauryn was using every precaution not to get detected. She knew that a regular phone could be tracked by cell phone towers. She also used cash to make most of her purchases. However, she continued to use her debit card for gas and other purchases. That would prove to be a grave mistake!

Lauryn had purchased a hijab to disguise both her and Sophia. She wanted to appear to be a Muslim. She had changed Sophia's name to Dreya. Lauryn had seemingly rehearsed everything down to the last detail. She did not know that an APB and missing person's report had been issued in Texas and several other states. The Cedar Hill Police Department was working on getting an Amber Alert issued. Detective Venti was taking the lead on getting the Amber Alert. It was a lengthy process.

Detective Venti spoke several times with Linda Forbes. Linda shared with the police that Lauryn was capable of causing great harm to Sophia, including killing her to prevent her dad from keeping her. Once Linda made those statements about Sophia's safety and potential death, an Amber Alert was issued in multiple states. We received several calls from Texas, Georgia, and other states sharing their concerns. Once the Amber Alert was issued, news broadcasts started carrying the story on the local and national news.

Many analysts were fearful that a person with Lauryn's profile would kill Sophia and then herself. This was a real possibility for Lauryn. She was on the run now. I knew that she was extremely impulsive. Several of my family members had come by our house once the Amber Alert had been issued. At least thirty television and radio stations were camped around our house.

After the Amber Alert was issued and Lauryn crossed state lines, the FBI took the lead along with the Cedar Hill Police Department. Lauryn had been detected using an ATM machine to get cash in Oklahoma. She had also spent the night at a hotel in Oklahoma.

Lauryn had less than a thousand dollars in cash in her account. We knew that Lauryn was trying to get to Illinois or Indiana, where many of her relatives lived. Lauryn drove with Sophia for the next day, until she entered the state of Indiana. She only stopped for gas. During every stop, she put on her hijab. She reminded Sophia of her newfound name, Dreya.

Her immediate family members had been contacted by the FBI and were told to contact the police if she was identified. The FBI had made contact with Lauryn again near Fishers, Indiana. A vehicle that she drove had been spotted. She parked near a local church that was pastored by her cousin. The SUV was hidden in the bushes near the church so that it couldn't be detected.

A few hours later, early on Sunday morning, Lauryn's vehicle was spotted near her cousin's house. The police and FBI knocked on the door. Lauryn's cousin opened it. The FBI searched the apartment. Lauryn was found hiding in a closet.

"Are you Lauryn?" they asked.

She said, "Yes, please don't shoot."

The search was over. Sophia was safe! The entire ordeal had only lasted four days, but it seemed like an eternity! News reports ran across the country about a young girl from Cedar Hill, Texas, who had been found safe in Fishers, Indiana. I got on my knees and thanked God for the victory.

Lauryn was transported to jail while Sophia was interviewed by the Indiana Department of Child Services for several hours. Detective Venti drove to Fishers, Indiana, to transport Sophia back home.

Redemption

I immediately took Sophia to see her therapist after she was returned home. She had been through too much for any child. After a few weeks in custody in Indiana, Lauryn was finally transported back to the Dallas County jail. I could not believe that Lauryn was finally in jail after many years of terrorizing my family and me. Crystal and I felt a deep sense of relief.

We also knew that Attorney Nimpson and Brian Benson were working vigorously to get her out of jail. The judge refused to set Lauryn's bail for several weeks. During a meeting with one of the former prosecutors in the case, I was told that Lauryn had been recorded making plans to leave Dallas County once she was released. She had made elaborate plans to leave the country and travel to Japan.

A few months into her stay in the Dallas County jail, Lauryn was accidentally released. It was our worst fear. We received notification by Detective Venti and a prosecutor that she was on the loose. We could not believe it! The Dallas County Jail accidentally released Lauryn! We were all in danger. They had released a woman who had been in FBI custody and arrested for kidnapping!

For the next several days, the Cedar Hill Police Department provided us with 24/7 protection. We had a police car stationed in front of our house. Sophia was escorted to school.

A few days later, we were notified that Lauryn had been found living with a friend in Dallas County. The U.S. Marshals found her in East Dallas. She was arrested and taken back to the Dallas County jail. We all breathed a sigh of relief.

Lauryn would stay in the Dallas County jail for a few months. We had hoped that she would stay in jail until the trial date. Her initial bail was set at over $300,000. We had hoped that Brian Benson would not post her bail again. After a few months, Lauryn was released on bail. We were not notified of her release. She immediately moved back to Atlanta to be close to Brian Benson. Once again, Brian had rescued her.

Lauryn was charged with two felony counts of interference with child custody and kidnapping. Lauryn was so good at getting out of trouble that we referred to her as Houdini. She had a keen ability to get out of situations that had killed most people. She had committed all kinds of serious crimes. She had been involved with street gangs during her teenage years. Her boyfriend had come up dead. She had severely burned a woman at a restaurant with scalding-hot grease. She had run several people off the highway. She had committed crimes in her early twenties that had landed her in jail. She had tormented Crystal and me for several years.

She had survived all this and had gone on to earn her master's degree and teach high school math at a prestigious high school in Atlanta, Georgia. She was dating two former NFL football players who met her financial needs and an attorney who was willing to support her in filing several false police reports.

Lauryn had lost her job and most of her possessions, but she was a fighter. She had survived a lot of adversity in her life. Brian was there to support her and bail her out when she needed help. She had been residing in one of Brian's rental properties in Atlanta. He allowed her to drive one of his vehicles.

Brian was obsessed with how he could fix Lauryn. He did not know borderline personality disorder cannot be "fixed." Treating it was difficult enough. Lauryn refused any treatment.

After her release from jail, Lauryn stayed at one of Brian's rental properties near Atlanta, Georgia. An argument ensued over Lauryn wanting Brian to rent her a car so that she could drive to Texas. Brian did not want to go on the trip with Lauryn. They had gone on other trips, and there were always major problems.

Lauryn started to cuss at Brian. "You Black motha f****, you can't get me a rental car so that I can see my family?"

This time, Brian left the house as Lauryn began to erupt. After leaving for a few minutes to calm down, Brian returned to his house to find that she had broken two doors and a glass table. She had thrown objects that left windows broken. Lauryn started to cuss at Brian and told him that it was his fault.

Brian yelled at Lauryn, "You are f****** crazy. Get some help. You destroyed my house."

Nothing would calm her down. As Lauryn continued to cuss and break items in his house, Brian left his house for a second time. Lauryn immediately followed Brian out of the house and got into her vehicle to chase him.

Lauryn pulled up behind Brian and hit the rear end of his car. The hit shook his vehicle and prevented him from leaving. Brian got out of his car and looked at the damage that was done. Lauryn continued to cuss and throw a temper tantrum.

After a few minutes, Brian returned to his house to get some personal items so that he could leave before even more damage was done. At that moment, Lauryn entered the house and grabbed a large brown paper bag and toilet paper. She lit the paper and threw the flaming bag underneath Brian's late model BMW.

Brian immediately threw water on the burning paper to prevent a possible explosion. Brian went into his home once again to try to get a few personal items before leaving. He was carefully watching Lauryn this time. He knew that she could be dangerous. Brian grabbed some expensive items from his home.

Lauryn grabbed him by the shoulders to keep him from leaving. She tore his shirt off and scratched him. Finally, Brian was able to get outside the house and put his treasured items in a neighbor's yard to get them away from Lauryn. She then got into her car and attempted to strike Brian with her vehicle. Brian jumped over a neighbor's fence to avoid being struck by Lauryn.

Brian barely missed getting hit. It had been many years since he had played professional football, but his quick reactions saved his life. Brian then got back into his car and attempted to get his property from his house. Seemingly out of nowhere, Lauryn grabbed a wooden two-by-four and struck the hood of Brian's truck, causing major damage.

As Brian left the house a third time, Lauryn tried to run him over again. She missed him and ran over the bushes in front of his house. As Brian tried to jump out of the way, he slipped in the bushes, and Lauryn hit his right leg, causing a laceration.

Brian immediately called the police as Lauryn yelled to him, "Don't f*** with me" as she tried once again to back him over with her car. When she missed hitting Brian, she sped away. The police arrived to find Brian with lacerations on his legs and scratches all over his back and shirtless. The officers witnessed the damage done to his car and home. The officers were able to retrieve burned pieces of paper, a broken kitchen knife, a sworn statement from a neighbor, and damaged property both inside and outside the home. Brian's neighbors had witnessed Lauryn's attempt to run Brian over multiple times.

I spoke with the prosecutor assigned to the case. I shared with him information about charges that Lauryn was facing in Texas. After our conversation, he worked diligently to get Lauryn prosecuted. He told me that Brian was not cooperating.

Brian received medical attention from paramedics. Several charges, including aggravated assault, were filed. The police immediately attempted to contact Lauryn and asked her to come in for questioning. She refused to come in without an attorney present. A warrant was issued for her arrest. Later that same evening, Brian contacted the police and provided a sworn statement, changing his story and asking that Lauryn not be prosecuted. Once again, Lauryn had avoided prosecution.

After many attempts by the prosecutor to get Brian to cooperate, he refused. All charges against Lauryn were dismissed. She had faced two felony charges of aggravated assault and two felony charges of criminal damaging property charges. All four charges were dismissed. She had escaped once again!

Verdict

Lauryn had been able to evade the justice system for many years. In early 2015, Lauryn would finally go to trial for the kidnapping and interference with child custody charges in Dallas County. A group of ethnically diverse jurors had been selected. Judge Hawk was the presiding judge. It would be an uphill battle to get justice for Lauryn's victims.

The past few weeks had been especially hard on Sophia. It was going to be difficult for her to testify during the trial. We discussed the issue for several weeks during therapy sessions. I encouraged Sophia to speak her truth. Not my truth or anybody else's, but her truth. I encouraged her to write down her thoughts. Sophia had been commended for her writing skills. She had written hundreds of pages of rap lyrics and poems. I was proud of her for making such positive strides.

As the day of the trial arrived, we had supported Sophia as best we could. During the first day of the trial, Lauryn had parked close to us. It was difficult for Sophia to see her mother under such conditions. Sophia had spent months in therapy. She had made so much progress. I was fearful that Lauryn would attempt to make Sophia feel sorry for her. Sophia looked stoic. Crystal, Linda Forbes, and Sophia's counselor, Karen, had done a great job preparing her for the worst.

After the jurors had been selected, the trial was finally getting underway. Judge Hawk asked Lauryn how she pleaded.

Lauryn said, "Not guilty."

The prosecuting attorney, Attorney Vance, began his opening statement: "Ladies and gentlemen, you sat through jury selection, and you may have come into this court thinking that you were going to hear some kind of a family feud, some kind of child custody dispute that has a lot of twists and turns. You are going to see that Lauryn Burns took Sophia from her home in Cedar Hill, Texas, and took her to Fishers, Indiana, where they were ultimately found by the police and FBI."

He continued, "This morning, you will hear from Gerald Ingram. He is Sophia's biological father. He's going to tell you that he followed the rules. He's going to testify about the court documents that he obtained and the process that he went through to have Sophia come live with him in Cedar Hill, Texas. And you're going to hear at every turn he followed the rules."

"Then you're going to hear from Sophia Burns-Ingram. You're going to hear that at the time she was taken from her home in Cedar Hill, Texas, she was twelve years old. You're going to hear that she was old enough to remember what happened, but you're also going to hear that she's young enough not to go against the will of her mother, that she's not going to fight her own mother. She's going to tell you that she went out to try and placate her mother. That she was surprised to see her mother in Texas at all. That when she went to placate her, her mother took her, convinced her that they were going for a short ride, and ultimately went for a longer ride. She is going to tell you that Lauryn had a suitcase already packed in her car."

"Sophia is going to tell you, 'Well, I wasn't ready to go on any kind of trip with my mother, because when I walked out of the house, I had no shoes on. I was wearing basketball shorts with no shoes.' She is going to tell you that she tried to convince her mother just to take her back but that her mother would not. That she kept driving, kept driving, kept driving. And that what turned from a short trip turned into an overnight stay in another state and ultimately ended up in Fishers, Indiana, with her mother hiding in a closet while the police came inside to try and find Sophia."

"You're going to hear from Crystal Ingram, Sophia's stepmother, who was there when Sophia was taken from Cedar Hill, Texas. She is going to tell you what she remembers, what she heard, what she saw, and that in no way did she believe when Sophia walked out the door, she wasn't going to see her for a couple of days."

"You're going to hear from law enforcement detectives from Cedar Hill. You're going to hear from the FBI here in Dallas and the FBI from Indiana. They will tell you efforts they undertook to track and ultimately find Lauryn in Indiana. Their effort in finding her, in conducting a nationwide Amber Alert. They will tell you that Lauryn was secreting Sophia and that she was taken with the intent not likely to be found. It was through their efforts that Sophia was found. And when you add those up at the end, you will find Lauryn guilty of interference with child custody and of kidnapping Sophia."

After the prosecuting attorney finished speaking, Lauryn's lead attorney, Ben Anthony, gave his opening testimony:

"Sophia is going to testify this morning. I am sure that she is conflicted. The evidence will show that when Sophia was contacted in Fishers, Indiana, she said that she wanted to live with her mother: 'I went with my mother and wanted to go with my mother.' She wanted to go! And on that basis, I think that you will find her not guilty."

"Sophia willingly left with her mother. She did not secret Sophia. You will find that Lauryn did not violate the law. She did not interfere with child custody proceedings. You will find that the Harris County orders are inconclusive. My client will be found to have only been a loving mother who did her best to see her daughter."

The attorneys continued to raise questions about the final court order awarding me primary custody. Attorney Anthony questioned the writ of habeas corpus that was issued out of the Harris County, Texas courts. Three orders were issued out of the Harris County courts on or about March 11, 2013. The Texas Courts would not accept the pickup orders from the Fulton County, Georgia Superior Court.

Attorney Anthony was attempting to make the case that the interference with child custody charge was invalid. He fervently questioned the legitimacy of Georgia's jurisdiction.

Attorney Anthony stated, "The reason that the principal in Harris County told them that they had to get a Harris County order is because the validity of the Georgia Court order has always been in dispute and it hasn't been resolved. If the jury is going to think that based on this Georgia order, the way it's been propounded, that he's got custody, and she violated the law by violating this order, this is not the order alleged in this indictment. To the extent that they're saying that this purports to be the final order that disposes of the issue, it's not. That's why they had to go back to Harris County. This Georgia order was an ex parte or default order."

Attorney Anthony continued, "I would ask the court to read the order. It is filled with all kinds of prejudicial language and findings that my client never had a chance to dispute. It's going to paint her in the worst kind of light and get into exactly the kind of abuse issues that we wanted to avoid in this whole trial."

He continued to question whether Lauryn had been properly notified of the Georgia proceedings prior to primary custody being awarded to me.

I learned very quickly that the legal process was not just about material facts. It was evident that Lauryn had been informed of every court proceeding in Georgia. When the Georgia courts started to turn on her, Lauryn ran to Texas in order to get sympathy from the courts. Her attorney was raising a lot of questions that I thought had already been answered in the court of law.

Attorney Anthony continued to question the service of process for Lauryn. He presented to the jury copies of the three orders issued from the Harris County courts. It was finally my opportunity to take the stand. After I was sworn in, Attorney Anthony began his questioning:

"There was an order to return the child on March 13th, correct?"
I stated, "Yes."
"Ultimately, it was signed by the judge of that court on March 14th, right?"
"That's correct," I stated.
"At the same time, there is an order for an issuance of a writ of habeas corpus. Is that right?"
"That's correct."
"Lauryn Burns is commanded to produce Sophia and have her before the court on April 2nd, 2013 at 9:30 a.m. Correct?"

"That's correct."

"That's signed on March 14th, 2013, correct?"

"Correct."

"Now, Lauryn Burns, the defendant—was she present for all this?"

"No, she was not."

"So, how did Sophia finally arrive in your possession? Did Lauryn bring her to you?"

"Linda Forbes, her godmother, actually brought her to the sheriff's department in Harris County."

"And Linda Forbes is a friend of Lauryn's, correct?"

"Yes, sir."

"Where was Sophia going to school when she came up here with you?"

"She was going to a middle school in Cedar Hill."

"Now, talking about April 11th, 2013, when is the first time that you heard that Sophia had been taken?"

"I heard about it that evening at 6:00 p.m. after my wife called me."

"What did you do when you got home?"

"When I got home, my wife was already talking to the Cedar Hill Police Department. I was told that Lauryn had taken her."

Attorney Anthony was doing his dead-level best to rattle me. The past fourteen years of struggling with Lauryn and trying to establish a relationship with Sophia kept coming to the surface. I felt a range of emotions. I was angry and fearful. I kept thinking about all of the people and systems that had failed Sophia.

Attorney Anthony continued, "I assume she's mentioned to you in some fashion that it's really uncomfortable bringing a child to court to have to choose between two parents, right?"

I almost lost it at this point. I responded, "I was not the one that caused us to be here in court this morning, sir. It is your client!"

I was angry and exasperated and Attorney Anthony knew it. He tried to get me to state for the record that I had coached Sophia.

"Did she tell you that she wanted to go with her mother?" Attorney Anthony asked.

"No, she didn't," I responded.

"She never said that?"

"No," I responded.

"She never expressed a concern about living with you?"

"No, she did not."

"She never said that she wanted to live with her mother basically her entire life, and she wanted to be with her mother? She never said that either?"

"No, sir."

The judge released me and admonished me not to discuss the case with anyone. Sophia was up next. I was nervous for her. She had stayed up many days and nights prior to the trial. I knew how difficult it was to give testimony. I had just told her to tell the truth and to speak from her heart and everything else would take care of itself. I knew that Attorney Anthony and his legal team would try to get her confused and tripped up on the facts.

The prosecutor, Attorney Vance, was the first to question Sophia.

"Can you introduce yourself to the ladies and gentlemen of the jury?"

"My name is Sophia, and I am fourteen years old."

"Are you nervous about your mom being here this morning?"

"Yes, sir."

"You still love your mom, do you not?"

"Yes."

"And some of what you have to say, it hurts you to have to say it. Is that true?"

"To a certain extent, yes, because that's my mom. But at the end of the day, I realize that I have to tell the truth."

"Now, you are a tall young lady. In fact, I was standing next to you, and I realize you're taller than me, but you're only fourteen years old. Is that right?"

"Right."

"Let's move right to April of 2013. Okay? So, when was the first time you talked to your mother that day?"

"I had called her."

"What did you all talk about?"

"Well, my stepmom had said that she had pulled up on her and stuff like that."

Attorney Vance said, "Let's slow down. I just want to make sure they understand who we're talking about. You're on the phone with your mother, right?"

"Yes."

"Did you have a cell phone?"

"Yes."

"Okay. So, you called her up, and your mom started crying, right?"

"Yes."

"So, where did you think that your mom was living at the time? Atlanta? Houston?"

"Well, I knew that she was in Dallas at the time, but I thought that she was in Houston prior to that."

"Okay. So, you heard that she was in town. Had you all planned a trip or anything?"

"No, sir."

"Did you expect her to be in Cedar Hill?"

"No."

"Okay. So, you're talking with her on the phone, and she said she wanted a hug?"

"Yes."

"Well, I mean, did you think that was okay for you to go out to see her?"

"Yes."

"Okay. Where did you see your mom?"

"Across the street from my house."

"Like in a driveway or street?"

"It was on the street."

"And she was in her car?"

"Yes."

"So, your mom called you and asked if you could come out and talk to her? Is that right?"

"No, give her a hug."

"Who were all in the house with you?"

"My stepmom and stepsister."

"What's your stepsister's name?"

"Megan."

"What's your stepmother's name?"

"Crystal."

"So, they're inside the house. Did you tell your stepmother that you were going outside to see your mom?"

"Yes."

"Did she approve of it?"

"She was following me, but I didn't think she was approving of it."

"When you went out to see your mom, what were you wearing?"

"I wasn't wearing any shoes, and I had on black shorts and a tank top."

"And when you get into your mom's car, can you tell everybody what happened?"

"I had gone into the passenger's side to give her a hug, and she pulled me in the car and rode away!"

"When you say she pulled you in the car, are you talking about a violent struggle?"

"Yes," Sophia replied in tears. She was starting to relive that momentous day. Her eyes started tearing up.

"Like, were you fighting her off?"

"Like, it was a violent jerk."

"What did you say to her?"

"I said, 'What are you doing?'"

"All right. What did she say?"

"She said, 'Oh, we are about to go to Sonic.'"

"Did you call anyone on your cell phone to tell them where you were going?"

"No. Actually, my stepmom called me first when she drove off."

"Because your stepmom was behind you just kind of watching what was going on?"

"Yes."

"So, what happened when your stepmom called?"

"When my stepmom asked me that, I was trying to tell her, 'Well, we're about to go to Sonic.' And my mom, she grabbed the phone from me, and she said, 'This is Sophia's mother. She's okay,' and hung up the phone."

"What did your mother say to you once you hung up the phone?"

"She said, 'Don't worry about that b****. You're with me now, so that's all you need to worry about.'"

"When did you realize that you weren't going to Sonic?"

"When we passed it, 'I thought we were going to Sonic.'"

"What did she say?"

"She said, 'Well, the cops might be there, and I don't want to go there and put myself at risk.'"

"What happened next?"

"My mom said that we were going to Red Lobster in McKinney. And I looked behind me, and I saw a suitcase. That's when I started to come to my senses. I knew I wasn't fixing to come back home."

"Did she ever use the phone with anybody?"

"Yes, with Matthew."

"Who was Matthew?"

"Her ex-boyfriend."

"Okay, and do you know what Matthew does for a living?"

"I think he's an ex-lawyer."

"Okay. Did you all ever stop for gas on April 11th?"

"Yes."

"How come when you stopped for gas, you didn't just jump out of the car and start running?"

"Because we were in the middle of nowhere."

"Did you want to be there with your mom on this long drive?"

"No."

"Did you all stop at a hotel?"

"Yes. We didn't stop for a hotel the first night, but we did on Friday night."

"How come you didn't just run and tell somebody that you didn't want to be there with your mom?"

"I was just confused and scared."

"So, let's talk about your mom at the hotel. What did your mom do when she got to the hotel?"

"She dressed up like a Muslim."

"And when you say dressed up like a Muslim, tell the jury what you mean."

"She put a scarf around her head like Muslim women wear."

"Did y'all watch TV in the room?"

"Yes."

"Did you see either yourself or something that you thought was about you on TV?"

"I saw at the bottom of the TV that it was an Amber Alert."

"When you saw the Amber Alert, did your mom say anything about that?"

"I said, 'Well, look, Mom, you know, this might be for me. You might as well, you know, take me home.'"

"What did she say?"

"She said, 'No, we can't do that. It's too late.'"

"Did your mom call anybody else?"

"Yes, she called my Aunt Karen in Chicago."

"What did she discuss with Aunt Karen?"

"She talked with Aunt Karen about finding a place for us to stay in Chicago."

Attorney Vance had done his dead-level best to get Sophia to tell the full story of what happened. She did her best not to look at her mom. Sophia knew the horrible things that had happened to her, but this was also her mother. Lauryn knew how to make Sophia feel guilty in order to gain her loyalty. It didn't seem to be working this time.

Attorney Vance resumed his line of questioning. "So, you and your mom wake up from the hotel early in the morning of Saturday, April 13th. Where did you all go next?"

"We went to a Wal-Mart."

"What did you go to a Wal-Mart for?"

"To get some shoes."

"So, you went without shoes on Thursday night, Friday, and until Saturday morning?"

"Yes."

"So, once you were in Wal-Mart, tell the jury why you didn't just yell out to somebody, 'Hey, I'm not supposed to be here,' or anything like that?"

"Because there were already cameras. I thought they would see me in the first place."

"Do you remember what state you were in?"

"Oklahoma."

"So, does your mom buy anything else in the Wal-Mart that you remember?"

"A prepaid phone."

"So, who does your mom call on the prepaid phone?"

"Her Uncle John in Indiana."

"What kind of conversation did she have with him?"

"I just remember her saying that she needed a place to stay."

"So, did you and your mom stop again to sleep or rest anywhere else?"

"Yes. We stopped at a rest stop and slept there."

"Did your mom ever ask you about changing your name?"

"Yes."

"What did she tell you?"

"She was saying for me to use the name Dreya."

"Do you ever remember stopping with your mom at, like, an ATM and you having to duck in the back seat?"

"Yes."

Attorney Vance offered several exhibits. The defense did not object. Sophia had been questioned for over three hours. She was starting to feel anxious.

"Was it at night when you met your Uncle John?"

"No, it was in the day."

"Did you watch TV at Uncle John's house, or see anything that made you think, 'Hey, people are looking for me'?"

"No. They actually ended up waking me up out of my sleep. I believe it was 2:00 a.m. or 3:00 a.m., and they told me they were after me. It was a nationwide Amber Alert. I walked into the room that morning, and the police were talking to Uncle John. My mom had put her sweater on and had hid in the closet. The police opened the closet door, saw her, and flashed a light on her and pulled her out of the closet."

Sophia had been on the witness stand for several hours. It was now the defense attorney's opportunity to cross-examine her. Attorney Anthony was a gifted trial attorney. He appeared unassuming, but he also had a sharp and biting wit.

"It sounds as though from direct examination that what you're telling the jury is essentially you felt like you were a prisoner the entire time. You just didn't want to be there. Is that correct?"

"Correct."

"Didn't want to get in the car at all."

"Correct."

"Really mad at your mom from the get-go about going there?"

"Yes."

"You wanted out at every opportunity?"

"Yes."

"Looking for a chance to escape but couldn't find one?"

"Right."

"Do you recall ever saying to anyone that when your mom was driving over there in Dallas to pick you up that you had a feeling that she was going to run with you?"

"Yes."

"Okay. So, as a matter of fact, before you ever got up to your mom's car, you knew she was coming to get you?"

"Oh, no. I knew I wanted to give her… I knew that she wanted a hug from me, but I didn't know that we were going to be on the run."

Attorney Anthony continued to try to trip Sophia up. Although she had been traumatized, she had a strong voice. Yet she felt conflicted. She wanted to tell her story, but she also wanted her mom to get help.

"Do you recall making a recorded statement in which you were asked the question if you wanted to go with your mother, and you said, 'Yeah, I wanted to go with her?'"

"No, sir."

"But if there is an audio recording on April 15th where you clearly state, 'To be honest, I wanted to go, I did, I did,' can those both be true?"

"No."

"I don't want to put words in your mouth, but it seems that you are extremely hostile toward your mother."

"No, sir."

"So basically, you're trying to tell the jury that you hate your mother?"

Attorney Vance quickly intervened, "Your Honor, I object to that question as argumentative."

The judge responded, "Sustained."

After Lauryn's testimony, Crystal was called to the witness stand. Attorney Vance began the direct examination of Crystal. "Obviously, you are here because Lauryn had a child in common with your husband, right?"

"Yes."

"Would you have known where she was living at that time in April of 2013?"

"No."

"Were you surprised to see her on your street that day?"

"Yes."

"Had you ever invited her to your house?"

"No."

"So, you saw her in her car on your street in Cedar Hill? What's the next thing that you remember?"

"I was coming to my house, and she was just parked two houses down. She was like in a curve in the street."

"So, who was in the car with you?"

"My daughter, Megan, and my niece, Brandy."

"What did you do next?"

"When I saw her, I needed to back up, because she started following me."

"So, instead of going home, where did you drive?"

"I drove through our neighborhood because I was a little afraid."

"So, you didn't want her to see you walk into the house?"

"No."

"How long did she follow you through the neighborhood?"

"Maybe five minutes. Our garage was in the back, so I just pulled into the garage."

"Was she still behind you at that time?"

"Well, she stopped me at one point. Like she pulled her car into me at one point."

"When you say 'into me,' what do you mean?"

"There was a car in front of me, and I stopped, and she drove her car close to me and looked into my car."

"What do you remember next?"

"I remember saying, 'Oh, my god.'"

"What do you remember after that?"

"I remember Brandy sitting there, stunned…saying, 'Oh, my god.'"

"Let's move to the point where Sophia was taken from your home and your street. Okay?"

"Okay."

"When did you first hear from Lauryn calling the house?"

"Sophia was on her cell phone."

"How did you know that she was on the cell phone with her mother?"

"She was on the speakerphone."

"So, what could you hear through the speakerphone?"

"'Where is Crystal? Where is Gerald? Am I being recorded?' That's how it started."

"What else did Lauryn say?"

"She started saying, 'Mommy, you're making Mommy sick. You don't want Mommy. I have been really sick, Sophia. I just want to hug you. We can go anywhere you want to go. Pumpkin, pumpkin, I love you. I'm never going to give up fighting for you.'"

"Okay. When she's asked about her coming out, wanting to give her a hug, do you give permission for Sophia to go out and give her a hug?"

"No. I told her not to go out."

"Okay. Does she go out anyway?"

"Yes, she does."

"What happens next?"

"Sophia is walking out the front door after I have gone to the bathroom. I was, like, twenty yards behind her. I was running behind her."

"Why were you following Sophia out there?"

"Because I was afraid for her."

"What do you see next?"

"I see her saying, 'Get in the car. Get in the car,' and pulling her into the car. I kept going toward her, but I didn't want to get shot. I know she has a gun."

Attorney Anthony interjected, "Your Honor, absolutely outrageous. We object to that and ask that the jury be instructed to disregard."

Judge Hawk responded, "Ma'am, only answer the questions that you are asked. I order the jury to disregard that last statement by this witness."

Attorney Anthony said, "I move for a mistrial."

Judge Hawk responded, "Denied."

The next witness was Detective Venti. Attorney Vance began his direct examination of Detective Venti.

"Detective Venti, can you tell the jury how you became involved?"

"I was assigned to be on call that weekend. I received a phone call that we had a possible child abduction and was requested to come to the police station."

"You ended up talking with the defendant Lauryn Burns, correct?"

"Correct."

"What was your conversation with Lauryn?"

"I was instructed that she was on the phone. As soon as I started talking with her, she was very agitated, very upset, and she told me that. I explained to her that we had a problem here, that she was being accused of abducting her daughter. She was very upset, saying she was not coming back, she was not giving her daughter up. I told her to come down to the police station so that we could discuss the matter and figure out this issue. She was very adamant that she was not coming back and that she was going to call her attorney."

"What did you do next?"

"A short time later, a person by the name of Matthew Nimpson called the police station. He asked to speak to me and referred to himself as her attorney."

"Did you speak with him?"

"Yes, sir."

And you say, 'her attorney,' correct? Did you find that they had a personal relationship?"

"I did."

"That he was, like, her boyfriend or something like that, correct?"

"I did."

"Did he attempt to try to get Ms. Burns to turn herself in to you?"

"He did."

"Was he successful?"

"No, sir."

"Can you tell the jury what other effort you took to find Lauryn?"

"That evening, we started to look at areas where she might be going. During my conversation with her, I heard road noise, so I knew that she was on a highway at a high rate of speed. So, I immediately started to look at relatives and friends and whoever I could possibly find that Lauryn would have gone to. We tried to obtain a ping on her cell phone to see if we could locate where she possibly was. We were able to get a nationwide Amber Alert issued the next morning. Shortly after the Amber Alert was issued, I got a phone call from the FBI telling me that they had full resources. They asked for a couple of subpoenas to be issued for cell phones to see if we could get some cell phone pings. We put a lockdown on her credit cards to see if they had been used, and we started to try to track her that way."

"When did you first hear that Lauryn may had been spotted?"

"We started getting calls from people saying that they spotted them here and spotted them there. The first really good spotting was a credit card that was used at an ATM. We obtained a video of the ATM transactions and could see Lauryn in the vehicle. And then I could see Sophia in the back seat. They were in Oklahoma at the time. We thought that she might be headed to Illinois because she had many relatives who lived in the area."

"Who ultimately spotted a car having to do with Lauryn? Who helped you out in that regard?"

"A police sergeant in Indianapolis, Indiana, called stating that they had identified Lauryn. She was eventually found in Fishers, Indiana. I drove to Fishers, Indiana, to pick Sophia up and transport her back to Cedar Hill the next day."

The next person to testify was Jim Lane with the FBI. Attorney Vance conducted the direct examination.

"Can you tell the jury when you were first assigned to anything having to do with Lauryn and Sophia?"

"It was early morning, April 14. I received a call from another FBI agent. She told me that an Amber Alert had been issued and that a vehicle had been located in Indianapolis that matched the Amber Alert description."

"What was the description of the vehicle?"

"It was a Ford Explorer."

"Someone had seen the car, given information on the Amber Alert hotline, and it was relayed to you, right?"

"Yes, sir."

"So, what did you do once the information was relayed to you?"

"I went out to surveil the vehicle and keep an eye on it."

"Where was the vehicle?"

"The vehicle was parked behind a shopping center in Indianapolis, Indiana."

"How long did you watch the vehicle?"

"I and my partner watched the vehicle for several hours."

"Did anyone come to the vehicle?"

"They did."

"What time did someone actually come to the car?"

"Shortly after 9:00 a.m. We saw an individual approach the vehicle on foot."

"Was it a male or female?"

"A male."

"So, a man comes and moves the vehicle from one place to another?"

"That's correct."

"Once the car is moved, what happens next?"

"The individual puts something into a gold Impala and parks the vehicle and then goes into the strip center for a few moments."

"So, they transfer some items from the car to the Impala?"

"Correct."

"And then they go inside to the presently being converted church?"

"Correct."

"What happens after that?"

"The gentleman exits the church, gets into the gold Impala, and then heads north."

"Do you follow the Impala or stay with the vehicle?"

"I followed the Impala to Fishers, Indiana."

"When they go to Fishers, Indiana, what do you recall happening?"

"The individual pulled into an apartment complex on the second floor. I then called local police officers to come for a uniform presence. We were in plain clothes."

"What happens next?"

"We go up and knock on the door, and a person named John answers the door."

"You identified Lauryn and Sophia in the apartment, correct?"

"Yes. We instructed Lauryn that she was under arrest for an outstanding warrant from Texas."

The next witness was Linda Forbes. She was Sophia's godmother. I fondly referred to her as the guardian angel.

"Do you know the defendant in this case, Lauryn?"

"Yes, I do."

"How long have you known Lauryn?"

"Since 1990-something."

"You've been friends for a long time?"

"Yes. She's one of my clients, and I work in a hair salon."
"Do you know Sophia?"
"Yes, I am her godmother."
"In March of 2013, where was Lauryn living?"
"In Georgia."
"And Sophia was living in the Houston area, correct?"
"Yes."
"And so, Sophia was living there, sometimes with her grandfather and a little bit with you, correct?"
"Yes."
"At some point, did you take Sophia to a police station to turn her—or surrender her to the police, and then ultimately to her father?"
"Yes."

Linda shared with the jury her conversation with the Cedar Hill Police Department prior to the Amber Alert being issued. She had been there for Sophia for thirteen years. The detectives had used Linda's statements to get the Amber Alert issued. She knew how dangerous Lauryn could be. She had risked her own safety to help Lauryn.

After Linda's testimony, the defense rested. The judge adjourned court until the next morning. The defense had made a strong case that the interference with child custody case should be dismissed. The primary argument was that Lauryn had not properly been served the final custody order. Attorney Anthony had made a strong case that the verdict should be made by the jury, not the judge.

The next morning, Judge Hawk determined that the interference with child custody charge was dismissed. This was a major blow to the state's attorney and his legal team. The kidnapping charge was the only charge left for the jury to determine guilt or innocence. One of the assistant district attorneys, Martha Benton, provided the closing argument for the state:

> On April 11, 2013, this defendant kidnapped Sophia Burns-Ingram, her own daughter,

by pulling her into a car and driving her all the way across four states, forcing law enforcement, including the FBI, to chase her down. To track her down, and then finally to come into an apartment where one of her relatives lives and arrest her in front of her own daughter, in front of this family. These are the defendant's actions and that is why we are here today, because she chose to do that, she chose to kidnap her daughter and she is guilty of kidnapping her daughter. I want to remind you that we talked about the elements of kidnapping and what the state would have to prove beyond a reasonable doubt in order to find her guilty of kidnapping her daughter. We had to prove to you that on or about April 11, 2013, in Dallas County, State of Texas, that Lauryn Burns intentionally and knowingly abducted Sophia Burns-Ingram, in that she restrained her by confining her and by moving her from place to place and by secreting and holding her in a place where she was not likely to be found.

You heard that she took Sophia and she confined her in that car, and she took her in that car from one place to another, from Texas to Oklahoma, from Oklahoma to Illinois, from Illinois to Indiana, one place to another. And she secreted her, and she held her in a place where she was not likely to be found. And you heard the police and the FBI testify to the efforts that they had to take in order to locate her. So, we have proven each and every element of that indictment beyond a reasonable doubt that she is guilty. I want to remind you that someone acts intentionally when it's their conscious objective or desire to engage in that conduct. If they want to do it, if they intend to do it, then they're intentionally doing it and it can be inferred by their actions. You don't have to have evidence of maps, or plans, or lists. You can decide in an instant to do something, and that is exactly what she did.

We had to prove that restraint is without consent. Without consent is, whenever it's accomplished by force, intimidation, or deception. We know that she used force, she grabbed Sophia into the car. We know that she intimidated her because Sophia said, 'I didn't feel like I could say anything.' And we know that she deceived her by telling her, 'We're just going to go to Sonic... We're just going to go to Red Lobster.' And she didn't go to Red Lobster. She went to Indiana. But there is another part of this that says that you can accomplish restraint by any means if the person—even if the victim agrees to go with you. Even if the victim acquiesces to the defendant, if she acquiesces to Lauryn wanting to take her into that car and go away with her, it's still without the consent of her father because the parent has not acquiesced. Gerald Ingram did not acquiesce to the child going with her, and the child is less than fourteen years of age. She had no ability to decide to go on a four-state road trip with her mother at all. She didn't have any choice in the matter. Her mother was driving that car. Her mother was driving that car with her shoeless and confused through four states.

This defendant intentionally and knowingly abducted her daughter, and she should be found responsible and guilty for those actions. The state rests.

The prosecutors displayed a profundity of the facts and a great deal of passion. I began to think that finally, the court system was going to work in our favor. We were cautiously optimistic.

The defense made its closing arguments. Attorney Anthony spoke for the defense:

I want to reiterate part of the charge that was read to you earlier by the judge. It says, 'In all criminal cases the burden of proof is on the state. All persons are presumed to be innocent and no person may be convicted of an offense unless each element of the offense is proved beyond a reasonable doubt.' It goes on to say that the presumption of innocence alone is sufficient to acquit the defendant unless the jurors are satisfied beyond a reasonable doubt of the defendant's guilt after a careful and impartial consideration of all the evidence in the case. I would like to talk to you briefly about how you determine what is credible evidence in this case. Your role is to decide if the state met every single one of its elements.

So, let's talk about the credibility of some of these witnesses. I'm going to start with Mr. Ingram. What do we know about Mr. Ingram? Well, what we know is that he wanted custody of Sophia, right? He would get a default judgment—which basically means Mom's not present—for custody of Sophia out of the State of Georgia. Then he proceeds to file a proceeding out of the 311th District Court in Harris County. But what did you learn? You learned that the case in Dallas had been transferred to a different court in Harris County, the 308th Court. So, Mr. Ingram proceeds to go to a court that does not have his case. He gets, at that point, ex parte orders. What does he leave the courthouse with? He leaves the courthouse with an order signed by a judge with a bunch of blanks in it that never, ever gets served on Mom. And what is that order? An ex parte order. An order for which Mom is not present. An order to which—so far, the mom hasn't been able to be present for anything, right? Where's the dad… the dad who wants custody of Sophia and is quite frankly willing to do whatever he needs to do without Ms. Burns being present?

So, this is the person, Sophia's father, who Sophia's been with for two years. And so, we are surprised when we hear Sophia's testimony now in 2015 versus the Sophia of 2013? We really shouldn't be surprised. She's been with him for two years. We hear, 'Mom jerked me into a car.' That's not what Sophia told CPS in Texas right after she was taken with them. Also, we hear the denial that she really, honestly wanted her mother to take her. We're talking a voluntary act versus reluctantly agreeing, right? And I would submit to you that means the state has not proven their case. Why would Sophia have wanted to go with her mom? She answered it today. She said right here today that she didn't know her dad. She said she had lived with her mom her entire life. Why wouldn't she want to go with her mom? Why wouldn't she voluntarily get in the car? Why would she cooperate with her mom and say, 'There are the police cars, we need to do this…There is an Amber Alert, we've got to do this'? Because she wanted to go with her? You heard Ms. Ingram's statement about walking out after Sophia starts walking toward her mom's car? And she starts following Sophia, and Sophia is speeding up to get away from her and get to her mom. Sophia was obviously wanting to get to her mom, not away from her.

So, you heard that Sophia had mixed emotions. Of course, she had mixed emotions. But mixed emotions are not an excuse for the State not proving their case beyond a reasonable doubt. You can't find people guilty of crimes when the state doesn't prove their case. And I would submit to you that Sophia voluntarily went with her mom, and that's what happened two years ago. Is it a good situation that happened? Of course not. But it is not kidnapping!

Attorney Vance responded:

May it please the court, I listened to what the defense had to say. By the end of it, I wonder if we even have the right person sitting at this table. Because you heard them go on and on about how it's everyone else's fault. It's everyone the state brought. It's their fault that we are even here. It's her stepmother's fault that she didn't restrain her and keep her from walking outside the house that day. It's twelve-year-old Sophia's fault that she was with her mother at the time. The defense wants to put them on par together, like, well, it was really Sophia's idea and she wanted to go with her if she would have made a different decision. They want you to make your decision based on the recollections and emotions of a twelve-year-old girl at the time, when there is a forty-three-year-old woman sitting here whose actions speak louder than any words. Go back and deliberate. Go over the evidence. Scrutinize the defense's case as well. They gave you twenty seconds of an interview. She was driven from Indiana all the way to Texas sleeping along the way in the car. She was immediately interviewed on the seventh.

The defense wants to put Sophia on par with her forty-three-year-old mother. Remember that the FBI had to conduct a stakeout to find her car and then follow a person who had moved her car to the house—now, you are entitled to have someone to come in and say that's not that big of a deal. That's not secreting, that's not hiding. She parked her car a twenty-minute drive away from where she actually stayed and let someone else go and unload it. An FBI agent had to sit in a car for hours watching it to find someone that moved it and then follow it to his home.

Gerald Ingram let Sophia go to school that day. When she came home and her mother took her, they did not hear from her again until the next Sunday. No phone calls, no hearing that she's okay. And somewhere in that, the defense wants to tell you, well, we can just throw up our hands and say this is somewhere between a crime and not a crime. If someone takes a child away from their home without shoes on, without their personal effects, when they know they're not supposed to take them, what else is it but a crime? And so, we brought you some of the evidence that just shows the intent of her actions. We knew she had a cell phone because you remember she called in McKinney on the cell phone. She said that we're going to Red Lobster. Well, why do you go buy a prepaid phone and now you start using that to call Uncle John instead of using your regular cell phone? Why did you do that? Because you did not want to get caught.

Start at the very end: They were in Fishers, Indiana—another state. Buying prepaid phones. Dressing up. Remember, Sophia covered her head up and pretended she was a Muslim so that they would not know who she was. Sophia said, 'My mom told me to go by the name Dreya.' You get to decide. If you think her actions were appropriate, if you think somehow this was okay, we can never convince you then. But what else is kidnapping except taking a child to another state and having to be found by federal law enforcement, the FBI. If that's not kidnapping, then kidnapping does not exist. We ask that you return a verdict of guilty.

Judge Hawk read the jury their instructions. The jury met for several hours. The judge allowed them to go home and deliberate the next day. Late that morning, the jury arrived at a unanimous verdict. Lauryn was found guilty of kidnapping!

We breathed a huge sigh of relief. The nightmare was finally over—at least we thought so. Lauryn looked back and whispered, "This is just round one."

We knew that it was not over. It was never over with Lauryn.

The sentencing hearing would be held a month later. The judge instructed Lauryn not to have any further contact with Sophia or our family while awaiting sentencing. It would be a long month. As we left the courthouse, Lauryn was attempting to make eye contact with Sophia and Linda Forbes. We all knew that Lauryn was vindictive and retaliatory. We knew that she took pride in silencing her enemies. "This was just round one," kept ringing in my head.

Justice

For the next several days, Sophia was constantly talking about the trial. She had mixed emotions about testifying in court. We discussed this with Sophia's counselor, Karen. She was able to help Sophia process the trauma that she had experienced over many years. I continued to take her to therapy to process the trial and its aftermath. I knew that she harbored some guilt.

Sophia had spoken her truth in her own words. Yet Lauryn had never said those magical words that she wanted to hear. "I am sorry. I apologize. Please forgive me."

Lauryn was too self-absorbed to say those simple yet powerful words so that Sophia could begin the healing process. I had encouraged her to speak her truth but to not say words that she would regret later. Her testimony was a sigh of relief for her. She finally had a voice. Not Lauryn's voice, but her own. I gave her the space to write and speak what was on her heart.

While awaiting the sentencing hearing, Lauryn and her attorneys filed a motion in Fulton County, Georgia, testing the validity of the Georgia Superior Court orders awarding me custody. Lauryn always fought on many fronts simultaneously. It was her way of controlling external events. Morality was never a part of how she viewed the world around her. It was all about winning at any cost.

Over the past two years, I had court proceedings in Fulton County, Georgia, and Dallas and Harris counties in Texas. I had hired five different attorneys over a period of two years.

I hired yet another attorney to represent me in Georgia. I had to fight for the courts not to vacate the order awarding me primary custody for Sophia. I flew to Georgia to meet with my new attorney and develop a legal strategy. We were going to fight the merits of

Lauryn's claims that she hadn't been properly informed of the court proceedings.

In the meantime, the sentencing hearing for Lauryn was held on March 9. Sophia's therapist, Karen, Crystal, Linda Forbes, Sophia, and the state's witnesses were present. The judge had ordered a comprehensive assessment and treatment services (CATS) evaluation. The courts were concerned about Lauryn's mental health.

During the sentencing hearing, Karen testified that Sophia had experienced physical and emotional abuse while living with her mother. Judge Hawk asked several penetrating questions to gather information on when and where the abuse had occurred. During my testimony, I stated the following:

Your Honor, I would like for you to consider some kind of jail or hospitalization for Lauryn for the sake of my daughter. It's not for me, it's for Sophia and my family's safety. It is for Sophia to have some semblance of peace until she's an adult. She at least needs to be removed from the community so that my family can feel safe after a fifteen-year reign of terror. Please stop the terror. Sophia's fourteen years old. She's been through a living hell. She's been tortured, and I don't use that term lightly—she's been tortured. And in my twenty-three years of working with troubled youth, I have never, ever seen a case like this. And so, I ask you to confine her because that will give Sophia some sense of peace, and I think it will give a sense of justice that you can't torture kids in the United States of America or in Dallas County. I think it will send a message.

Judge Hawk asked the question, "Can you explain the torture part to me?"

I responded:

Let me explain to you some examples that Sophia has written down in her journal. She has been confined in her house when she lived in Alpharetta, Georgia. She lived by herself for days at a time, calling only her godmother. She reported incidents where Lauryn would sit on her until she vomited. Lauryn would put her in a plastic bag, and she could barely get out of the plastic bag—but she found a way out. She was beaten several times. Lauryn put feces in her face. The list goes on and on and on. And I reported this to child welfare agencies in both Texas and Georgia on numerous occasions. There have been some horrific things that have happened to her, and that's why I say that it's torture. It's not abuse, it's torture. And that's just a few of the incidents. I could give you an additional fifteen incidents that Sophia has told me about. She has threatened to cut Sophia's body up and send the head to Texas and leave her body in Georgia.

Judge Hawk continued to ask me why I hadn't called the police. I told her that I had contacted the police numerous times, but I was directed to call CPS and file a report. Once the reports were filed, investigations were never conducted to my knowledge. The only time that a thorough investigation was conducted was after the Amber Alert and years ago when I was accused of neglectful supervision. I was often asked how this could happen without the "authorities" taking more action. My response was that public systems often fail children. The signs are often obvious. There were many "mandated reporters" that failed in their obligation to report what was happening to Sophia.

This is not uncommon, especially for parents or guardians who threaten to do harm to their children. The children often suffer in silence while the adults often go unpunished. So often, the burden is left on the kids themselves to report what happened to them. If there is no "outcry," kids are often abused without any system response. Traumatized children are often incapable of sharing their story for fear of retaliation. The cycle of victimization and retaliation leaves far too many children in a vicious cycle of abuse.

Sophia had waited many years for a chance to tell her story. She had spent days writing her testimony. Sophia shared the following in her testimony:

Throughout the twelve horrific years of living with a delusional, demented, erratic, and manipulative monster, I know that you are probably wondering why I have so many strong feelings of animosity and hostility toward her. Ever since I could remember, I was constantly beaten, choked, and violated by this woman. I played the role of many things besides her daughter. I played the role of her punching bag, her therapist, her lover, and her internalizer. I never had a chance to enjoy my childhood because of the way I was treated. I was an animal. My house was my cage, and my mom was my owner. I was my mother's property. I was her slave. I was her possession, and I was her servant. I never really could understand why my mother treated me the way that she did.

I remember when I accidentally interrupted her on the phone, and she came in my room naked and began to choke me in my sleep. As I tried to run, she said, 'b**** be still,' and repeatedly punched me. And the thing that irritates me so much about it is that she enjoyed the pain that was inflicted on me! I also remember another incident when she beat me because I didn't understand my homework. She gave me ten seconds to get the answer right, and if I didn't, I would get beat over, over and over. She also made me take all my clothes off in the process. After beating me, if I didn't put my panties on in five seconds or less, I would get beat even more. The beatings were countless and felt never-ending. Once the beating was over, I was left with blisters all over my legs and back. My skin was ripped open, blood oozing down each side of my legs so badly I was forced to wear long-sleeved shirts and pants. And I wasn't able to interact with kids just in case anyone grew suspicious.

When I was six, I also recall another incident. At school, I would get in trouble because I would cuss kids out. That was only because I was acting out what my mom was saying to me. Anyway, my behavior had gotten so bad, I had to get sent home. My mom's punishment was to sit on me so I could be still. She beat me, punching while laughing. Once again, this would bring pleasure to her. Eventually, I threw up because of the pressure and weight on my body. She didn't even care. She got her last few punches in as she got up and told me, and I quote, 'clean up that mess from my floor, b****' And I did what I was told.

And, yeah, I know what you're thinking, 'Why didn't you say anything?' That is a good question. I didn't say anything because I was manipulated into thinking that every other kid had to go through the same thing that I did. She referred to this as discipline. Or at least her sick way of thinking of it.

Another incident that I remember is the November 9 situation, which happened when I was eight years old in 2008. My mother was in the bed and told me that she was cramping real bad and to leave her the f*** alone. I did what I was told. But soon enough, I came back into my mom's room. I recall asking her what was wrong. She replied, 'b****, I told you to leave me the f*** alone. Get the f*** out of my room before I kill you, b****.'

I said, 'Yes, ma'am,' and left. As I went by, I still wanted to see what was wrong with my mom. But this time she had a different response. She jumped up and began choking me down the stairs. She then jumped up on me and yelled, 'Die, b****, die! I wish I had an abortion, b****… F*** you,' she repeated.

She gripped on tightly to my throat as I was gasping for air. I kept on fighting, trying to get loose from her grip, and started running upstairs. But instead of chasing me, she calmed down and brought me to her room. She told me how she would love to chop my head off and keep it in Texas and the rest of my body in Georgia. She also said how much she hated me and how much she wished she never f***** my dad. As she was telling me this, she came up behind me and started choking me once again and started screaming, "Die b****! Die, b****! Die, b****," and she slobbered and drooled all over my face. The next thing that I know was that I woke up in a trash bag. My legs were halfway out of the trash bag. Once I got out of the trash bag, I saw my mom in the restroom panicking, trying to find out what she was going to do next.

When my mom realized that I had escaped out of the trash bag, she grabbed the closest thing to her, which was the scissors, and she began chasing me once again. This time, I grabbed the phone and ran outside and threatened to call 911. She dropped the scissors and said, 'I'm done with you b****. Take your mothaf****** a** to bed.' Now, Judge, I know you are thinking that this is unrealistic and unbelievable, but growing up with this woman, this was a normal day for us.

Another incident that I would like to address would be the 'poop' situation. I believe that the year was 2011, and we were living in our new townhome, which was two levels. One day, my mom noticed that the downstairs toilet was not working. Therefore, she told me not to use it. One day, when I was coming home from school, I had to use the restroom real bad. Forgetting that the restroom downstairs was having problems, I continued to use it. When I flushed the toilet, it began to overflow. My mom came downstairs and proceeded to beat me once again. Then she demanded that I stick my hand into the toilet and put it on the floor. Feces were all over my hands and was in my fingernails. I dug so much out of the toilet that the stench of it burned my nose.

Next, my mom grabbed a plunger and put the poop on the plunger and put it in my face. As I was crying, she told me, 'Stop being a b****.' She then told me to swallow my spit because she didn't want to get her floors dirty. She also began laughing and calling my family members and telling them about my punishment. Once she was done talking to her family, I had to clean up the mess. I picked up all the poop before I could even take a bath and clean myself up.

On a different note, I could never have a father figure because of her misconceptions of me. One time, my mom's boyfriend, Brian, was flying in from Atlanta to Houston so that he could visit us. Once they arrived, I gave Brian a big hug. My mom quickly became agitated. She pointed at the shorts that I had on and how they were 'slutty'-looking. I asked, 'What are you talking about? The shorts are barely even past my knees.' She then told me not to talk back to her and to change while Brian was using the bathroom. My mom burst open my door and began to say, 'You're a slut. That's my d***. You want him to stick that fat d*** inside you, whore, then do it.' She then made me take off all my clothes and walk right outside the restroom door.

She then began saying to Brian: 'Come out, Brian, and get some young p**** waiting right here.' Brian didn't reply. After waiting for five minutes for Brian to come out, she told me to change into some pants. The next day, she acted like nothing had happened.

In my closing points, I want to make some brief statements. First, I deserve justice. For everything that this woman has put me through. She took away my sense of dignity and, most importantly, my childhood. Because we were too busy trying to duck and hide from my dad. My whole life, she manipulated me into thinking my dad was the delusional one, when it turns out, she was the crazy one the whole time. And she blinded me to the point where I believed it. I was her robot. She was my pimp. She was anything besides a mother. And my dad continues to do everything that she failed to do. He is the most compassionate, sweetest, most down-to-earth man in the world. And how could a woman like her keep me from him?

And to you, Judge, just know that this is a show. It is a manipulative game that she is playing with you. And I am begging you not to fall for it. Please let me and my family have a sense of peace and freedom for the first time. We want to be happy. She's not going to stop. Please hear me out! And as for you, Lauryn Burns, I wish you the best, and I hope you get the help that you need. But I do hope that you get time. People like you don't deserve to roam the streets and be free. And I have chosen to forgive you for my own good. But eventually, I hope you accept and respect that I'm happy now. And I'm not going to let you mess this up. And at the end of the day, we both know what happened throughout those horrific years. You know what you did, and that's all that matters.

The room was silent for several seconds.

Judge Hawk said in a slow, monotone voice, "I believe you. I believe you. If nobody else believes you, I believe you. Did you write those words, Sophia?"

"Yes, I wrote every word."

After further exchange between the attorneys, Judge Hawk spoke directly to Lauryn Burns,

"I think you want everything your way, and I think you've taken out all your frustrations out on that poor little girl, and that pisses me off because I am the last person that can protect a child. And that's why my intention, in this case, is to keep her from you. She's old enough now that she can decide who she wants to live with, and if she wants to live with you, she can come live with you, but if she doesn't want to, then by God, you better leave her alone."

After the hearing was over, Judge Hawk walked down and spoke with Sophia. She gave her a big hug and said, "I believe every word that you said."

Sophia was crying profusely as the judge gave her these words of affirmation. She had finally been heard and believed.

A few weeks later, Judge Hawk sentenced Lauryn to a ten-year suspended sentence. She was mandated to serve on a mental health probation caseload. The judge allowed her to return to Atlanta. This would prove to be a huge mistake. The CATS assessment had shown that Lauryn was both a threat to herself and others. She was both homicidal and suicidal. Lauryn was not stable enough to remain in the community. The judge had released her against the advice of mental health professionals.

Sophia's voice had finally been heard and believed by Judge Hawk. That was all that really mattered. Lauryn rolled her eyes at Sophia, Crystal, Linda Forbes, and me as she left the courtroom. We knew this wouldn't be the end. The end was never the end with Lauryn Burns. She gave the look that signaled that the battle was not over.

Lauryn was allowed to return to Georgia without court or probation supervision. The judge had known about the prior cases in Georgia when Lauryn had stabbed and assaulted her boyfriend. She had been arrested twice for kidnapping and filing false police reports. The judge had the option to hospitalize Lauryn, but she allowed her to roam free while the case was on appeal.

After many years of working with children, I made the false assumption that courts did everything in their power to protect the interests of children, especially when a child had experienced such extensive abuse. I was wrong, at least in my case!

After the sentencing hearing, I felt a sense of relief, but also unease. I knew that Lauryn would seek revenge. I knew that she could not deal with loss. She had always won. I knew that she would retaliate. The end was never the end with Lauryn.

No Way Out

Lauryn's reign of terror had continued unabated since 1999. She had terrorized many people over the years. She had killed, injured, maimed, harassed, threatened, and physically harmed countless people. Sophia had been her worst victim. For twelve years she had dealt with continuous abuse from Lauryn.

We knew that Lauryn was not stable enough to live in the community. She had terrorized hundreds of people over many years. She refused to get treatment for her mental illness.

Judge Hawk allowed Lauryn to return to Atlanta while other cases were pending in Dallas County and Fulton County, Georgia. This was a mistake of epic proportions. Lauryn had demonstrated that she could not be released from jail without jeopardizing the lives of others.

The Amber Alert two years earlier. The false police reports. The physical abuse. The assessments that Lauryn was suicidal/homicidal. The testimony of the arresting FBI officer. The statements of licensed professional counselors. The psychiatric evaluations. Judge Hawk overlooked all this history and allowed Lauryn to return to Atlanta. I was outraged! I knew that she was capable of doing anything. The mental health professionals and detectives knew it too!

I was fighting two appeals in two different states. Brian Benson had paid for high-powered attorneys to represent Lauryn in the Georgia courts. He made a strong case that the original Texas order issued in 2004 was not transferred to Georgia properly.

Lauryn was a survivor. She knew how to project an image of strength even when she was vulnerable. She also knew how to attract men with money. She was now dating two ex-NFL football players at the same time: Frank Barnes and Brian Benson. She had been dating both men for the past few years. They helped her with her dwindling finances, but they could not help her emotional and psychological state.

I attended the court hearing in Atlanta in March of 2015. After weeks of deliberation, the presiding judge ordered that the custody orders awarding me custody in the Georgia courts could stand! This was another major victory. Two courts had ruled in our favor within a matter of weeks. We celebrated the victory!

I had spent well over $250,000 in legal fees since meeting Lauryn Burns in 1999. The greater expense was the psychological and emotional cost to Sophia and my family.

It had been an uphill battle, but at least we had finally won a conviction against Lauryn. My family and I had just wanted the reign of terror to end. It had taken fifteen years to get a semblance of justice.

I had learned how difficult it is for a Black man to get justice in America firsthand. I had personally witnessed how the systems that were supposed to protect children failed my daughter and me. I had learned that the legal notion of "presumption of innocence" far too often didn't apply to Black men. There is far too often a "presumption of guilt."

The criminal justice, child welfare, public school, and other public systems didn't work as they should have. I had met with prosecutors, sheriffs, detectives, guardians ad litem, attorneys, school administrators, child protective services administrators, judges, attorneys general, and others to help my daughter. I had spent a lifetime working with those systems to improve outcomes for vulnerable young people, but I found them all to be terribly broken. They didn't work as they ought.

After the appeal in Georgia, I felt that Lauryn had exhausted her legal appeals. Lauryn was full of surprises. Brian was keeping her from being homeless. She didn't have any income. She had lost her job as a teacher. The appeal of the kidnapping conviction in Dallas County did not have a strong likelihood of being overturned.

Lauryn faced other charges related to her filing false police reports in Dallas County. She had filed over twelve false police reports with the help of her attorney, but now, her deception was coming to an end. Lauryn was broke and desperate. She had lost the things and persons most important to her.

Lauryn really wanted Brian Benson all to herself. She had stabbed him, almost run him over, attempted to blow up his car, threatened his wife many times, and broken and stolen his property. Yet Brian Benson and Matthew Nimpson were still there for her through thick and thin. I don't know if they stayed with her out of fear, love, or both.

For a few months after the sentencing hearing, it was quiet—too quiet for comfort. Lauryn had to check in with her probation officer in Texas on a frequent basis. My family and I were fearful that Lauryn would strike at any time. I was also fearful for Sophia's godmother, Linda Forbes. Linda had been a constant source of support for Sophia for many years. She and her family had taken a major risk by testifying against Lauryn.

We knew that Lauryn was busy plotting against us. Early in the morning on June 29, 2015, Crystal and I were home. I was at my home office on a conference call. Crystal looked over her left shoulder through the window and saw a black sports utility vehicle parked not far away from our home. The person was using binoculars. She looked strikingly similar to Lauryn.

We immediately contacted the police while I got in my vehicle and attempted to follow her. I immediately contacted the court to make them aware that Lauryn was within a few yards of our home. The court had informed Lauryn not to be within five hundred feet of our property as part of the condition of her release.

I knew that Lauryn possessed a gun. She had lost everything and everyone that mattered to her now. I knew that we were her targets, but I always felt a sense of divine protection for my family and me.

I personally spoke with Judge Hawk a couple of days later. I shared with her my frustration that Lauryn had been released from jail.

"She should have at least been confined in a psychiatric facility," I told Judge Hawk emphatically. I also sent Judge Hawk a long e-mail detailing to her why releasing Lauryn was putting a lot of people in danger. She appeared sympathetic. She told me that she would have Lauryn appear in court within a matter of days. I called Linda Forbes and told her that Lauryn was back in Texas and to be careful.

Brian Benson continued his relationship with Lauryn. Brian was married to a compassionate, accomplished woman who taught students with special needs. She was fiercely in love with Brian. She had known about Brian's affair with Lauryn. Lauryn had called her numerous times and told her that Brian was "her man." Lauryn had harassed Sandy for months.

Lauryn had done the same thing to Matthew Nimpson's wife and to Crystal. Lauryn always targeted the wife or girlfriend. In her mind, she had to get the woman out of the way so that she could have the man all to herself. Lauryn desperately wanted to get Sandy out of the way so that she could have Brian all to herself.

After many years spent in an affair with Lauryn, Brian reluctantly told Lauryn that he was going to reconcile with his wife, Sandy. They planned to go on a trip to rekindle and reconcile their broken marriage. Sandy was excited. She had always loved Brian unconditionally.

After Brian revealed to Lauryn his plans to reconcile with Sandy, she became enraged. Lauryn met Brian at his job on the morning of July 15, 2015. She was seething with anger after Brian told her about his upcoming trip with his wife. After a few minutes of arguing, Lauryn told Brian, "I am going to kill that b****." Brian didn't take her warning seriously.

At approximately 11:20a.m. that morning, Lauryn drove to Sandy Benson's home.

Lauryn yelled, "Open this door! Open this door, or I'm going to kill you."

Sandy's longtime friend was on the phone with her as Lauryn pounded on the door.

Sandy eventually opened the door with her friend on the phone. As she opened the door, Lauryn pointed a revolver at Sandy.

Sandy yelled, "Don't hurt me, ma'am. I don't know you. Are you Lauryn Burns?"

Lauryn pulled Sandy at gunpoint into Brian's black Dodge Durango that he had given to Lauryn. Once in the vehicle, Lauryn pulled out handcuffs and tape that she had purchased just minutes earlier. She put Sandy in the back seat and sped off.

Immediately, Sandy's best friend and a neighbor called the police. Brian was contacted immediately. He attempted to call Lauryn. After several attempts, he was able to reach her. Lauryn had a range of emotions as she spoke with Brian. She said, "I am going to kill this b****." one moment. A few minutes later, she was talking about having sex with Brian. Sandy listened as Lauryn made her feel inept as she was handcuffed in the back seat. Lauryn tortured Sandy for several hours.

"You see? He is my man now," Lauryn screamed at Sandy.

Whenever Lauryn was not talking to Brian, she was on the phone with her father. Lauryn's dad had given her the handgun that she used to kidnap Sandy. Lauryn and her father had a toxic relationship, but he always felt that he had let her down. He had supported Lauryn's unhealthy relationships. He had been in court supporting her while she was on trial in Dallas just a few months earlier. He was trying his best to keep her from doing the unthinkable.

Now he was fighting to save his daughter's life.

"Lauryn, please put the f****** gun down. Please, Lauryn. Everything is going to be okay."

"I'm tired, Daddy. I am tired of fighting. I have lost everything. I have lost Sophia. Lost Brian. Lost everything. I don't have nothing to lose, Daddy."

Brian was working with the police to find the exact location of Lauryn and Sandy. During one of the calls, Lauryn allowed Brian to speak to Sandy. Lauryn placed the phone near Sandy's mouth, but all that she could hear was mumbling. Her mouth was still taped shut.

Brian could hear Sandy say in muffled words, "I love you with all my heart."

Lauryn had started to act like a child. When in stressful situations, Lauryn would often revert back to childhood. She would baby talk. She would become angry one moment and submissive the next. Sophia often described Lauryn as acting like Barney or other characters. I would later wonder if Lauryn also suffered from dissociative identity disorder.

Lauryn's father was in frequent contact with her by phone while Lauryn drove at high speeds to evade the police. It had been several hours, and the police had not located her. Lauryn had a master plan. She wanted to pay Brian back for his deceit. Once again, she wanted to eliminate the women who stopped her from having Brian all to herself. Lauryn contacted one of Brian's other girlfriends who lived in Mississippi. Lauryn had plans to kidnap and kill her as well.

Brian called to give her advance warning not to answer the door. He spoke to the woman's husband that he had been having an affair with. It saved her life. Had she answered the door, she might have been shot and killed or kidnapped. Lauryn was desperate. Lauryn stopped at a convenience store. Sandy had been detected on camera. She allowed Sandy to walk with her into the stores. Sandy was understandably too frightened of Lauryn to ask for help.

Lauryn had been on the run for over twenty-four hours. She had held Sandy hostage and tormented her. Lauryn was talking back and forth with her father and Brian. They were both trying to get her to release Sandy. The police had finally located Lauryn. She had a critical decision to make. She would be facing many years in prison if arrested. She had spent several months in jail in Texas and Indiana. That was not an option for her. While she had imprisoned others, she could not face prison herself.

A detail of several police cars trailed Lauryn as she drove down highway 20 from Georgia into Alabama. Lauryn was desperate. She was impulsive and deranged.

She told her father, "I love you, Dad. It's over."

Lauryn slammed on her brakes in the middle of Highway 20 in Alabama near mile marker 208 in Cleburne County, Alabama.

Lauryn said to Sandy, "This is for taking my man."

Lauryn pulled the trigger and shot Sandy in the head. She died immediately. A few seconds later, Lauryn placed the revolver against her right temple and pulled the trigger. She slumped over against the driver's side window. It was over!

A police chase that had begun a day earlier had ended in a murder-suicide. The police would later find that Lauryn had receipts indicating the shops where she had purchased tape, handcuffs, ankle cuffs, pepper spray, a kitchen knife, and a box of .38 special live rounds days earlier. Lauryn always planned things ahead of time.

To those of us who knew her, it was no surprise that it had ended this way. I heard the news on Thursday night, July 16. I was at home that evening in bed.

Sophia came running to the bedroom door, yelling, "My mom is dead. My mom is dead."

Crystal and I did not believe her. Some of Lauryn's family members had reached out to Sophia and told her that her mom had been killed. They didn't have the details at the time.

My daughter had lost her mother. I was angry that Judge Hawk hadn't placed her in a psychiatric facility or jail. She had been allowed to roam free. An innocent woman who had spent her career working with special-needs children was needlessly dead. Sandy's family would later find that Brian was aware of the threats Lauryn had made. Did Brian have a role to play? Was he complicit in any way? Did he cooperate with Lauryn to have his own wife killed? A civil suit was later filed to get Sandy the justice that she deserved.

Of course, Brian had placed his wife in a harmful situation. Why hadn't he responded to Lauryn's threats to kill his wife? Why didn't he at least check on her that morning? Why did he expose his wife to such danger in the first place? These are all questions that will probably never be answered.

Lauryn's family decided not to have a funeral. Many of Lauryn's family members were angry that Sophia had testified in the kidnapping case. Many of them blamed Sophia for her mother's death.

I decided to have a private memorial for Lauryn in our home. It was the least we could do for Sophia. We invited Lauryn's sister, Tina, and her children. She had always been supportive of Sophia. After the memorial, we released balloons at Prayer Mountain.

A Final Word

Lauryn's reign of terror ended in a murder-suicide. This outcome could have been prevented. We were deeply saddened, but not surprised. We knew that things would not end well. We also knew that Lauryn was not well.

Once I heard the news, I immediately called Judge Hawthorne (Judge Hawk in the book) and told her the news. Just a few weeks prior, I had informed Judge Hawthorne that Lauryn was sighted near our home with binoculars. She had planned on killing my wife, stepdaughters, and me. She was trying to figure out how to kill us without injuring Sophia. My wife immediately called the Cedar Hill Police Department. A police car was stationed in front of our home for several days. Even after this incident, Judge Hawthorne refused to confine Lauryn in jail. She was released with no form of supervision, even though a risk-assessment instrument stated that she was both homicidal and suicidal.

Lauryn left behind a litany of victims across Texas, Illinois, Arkansas, Alabama, Georgia, and possibly other states. All of this could have been prevented if the courts in Texas had hospitalized her or confined her while she was filing for an appeal on her conviction for kidnapping. The courts should have confined Lauryn after she severely burned a woman at a fast-food restaurant when she was in her early twenties. The lack of intervention led to her unbridled rampage through multiple states.

I have spent the past thirty years working to develop alternatives to incarceration for youth and young adults across many states. I never thought that I would be the victim of the very systems that I had partnered with to develop safe and effective community-based alternatives for young people.

I am blessed to work for an employer (Youth Advocate Programs Inc.) that supported me throughout the ordeal. I am especially grateful to the late Tom Jeffers and to Minette Bauer and Jeff Fleischer.

It is my hope and fervent prayer that this book will help those who are dealing with mental illness themselves, have loved ones who may need help, or have responsibility for supporting those with mental illness. I hope that this book will lead to deeper conversations about how untreated mental illness negatively impacts the lives of far too many children, youth, adults and their families.

According to the National Association for Mental Illness (NAMI), one in five adults experience mental illness each year. One in twenty-five adults experience serious mental illness each year, and one in six children and youth ages six to seventeen experience a mental illness each year. Approximately 1.4 percent of people in the United States are estimated to have BPD. The number may be as high as 5.9 percent.

NAMI lists the following symptoms of BPD:

- Impulsive behaviors that can lead to dangerous outcomes, such as excessive spending, unsafe sex, substance abuse, or reckless driving.
- Efforts to avoid real or imagined abandonment by friends or family.
- Unstable personal relationships that alternate between idealization ("I'm so in love!") and devaluation ("I hate her!").
- Distorted and unstable self-image.
- Chronic feelings of emptiness.
- Inappropriate, intense, or uncontrollable anger—often followed by shame or guilt.
- Dissociate feelings—disconnecting from your thoughts or sense of identity, "out of body" types of feelings, and paranoid thoughts and brief psychotic episodes.
- Periods of intense depression, irritability, or anxiety.
- Self-harm behavior, including suicidal threats or attempts.

Lauryn exhibited many of these symptoms over the years, combined with schizoaffective characteristics. I am not a mental health professional, but it was clear that she had some serious mental health challenges that threatened her safety and the safety of others. I fervently believe that mental illness alone should not be the sole factor in determining which parent should have primary custody of a child. It is evident in Lauryn's case that she did not have the mental capacity to care for Sophia.

I am hopeful that judges, prosecutors, public defenders, psychologists, psychiatrists, court administrators, social workers, school personnel and administrators, guardians ad litem, coaches, therapists, and the public at large will do more to protect and support vulnerable children. In family courts across the country, tens of thousands of vulnerable children are involved in court proceedings that will determine their future well-being.

In no way do I believe that removing children from their parents is the best solution. In fact, far too many children are removed from their relatives in the United States. I believe that we place too many children in foster care, residential treatment facilities, and secure detention centers. We need to provide better support and resources to parents and other caregivers in their own homes.

I have often been asked, "What do you suggest could be done so that other people do not have to experience what you and your family did?" My response is, too often, children who are in abusive situations don't have a voice even when they make an outcry. Often, the parents who speak the loudest and "strike first" get the family courts and law enforcement on their side. Lauryn would always strike first. The law enforcement system in Dallas would arrest first, often with no factual basis. A series of false affidavits could have led me to prison. That should not happen in America. The legal aphorism of "innocent until proven guilty" or "presumption of innocence" did not apply to me and countless other people of color.

I have always been consumed with "what if" questions. What if I hadn't signed an affidavit of non-prosecution against Lauryn in the fall of 1999? What if the police had intervened after Lauryn struck herself in the stomach while she was carrying Sophia? What if CPS had intervened when Sophia was just a week old and Lauryn almost drowned her? What if I had been home on the day that Lauryn kidnapped Sophia? What if someone other than her godmother had spoken up for Sophia? What if Judge Hawthorne had confined Lauryn after the kidnapping conviction rather than releasing her to return to Georgia? Would any of this have made a difference?

Ultimately, the family courts, criminal justice system, Child Protective Services, schools, and many other professionals failed to respond properly. Beginning in 2011, the Georgia family court system was responsive. They appointed a guardian ad litem and took Sophia's safety seriously. They didn't buy into Lauryn's false allegations. Lauryn often would appear in court without Sophia being present. She would submit to the court letters that Sophia had allegedly written. Lauryn had written them. The letters often made me out to be the bad guy.

I thank Judge Dorsey, Attorney Karen Brown-Williams, Attorney Cantu, Attorney Tiffany Harvey and Attorney Diana Lynch for their excellent work and persistence in the State of Georgia. There were school personnel both in Texas and Georgia who cared deeply. They weren't immobilized by fear as so many other professionals were. I knew that their hearts were in the right place.

What can be done to prevent such "system failures" from happening to other children and families? Courts, prosecutors, Child Protective Services, schools, guardians ad litem, attorneys, and law enforcement officials should be trained in identifying characteristics and symptoms of mental illness. Many law enforcement officials are already trained in how to deal with persons with severe mental illness. My experience is that judges and prosecutors are not aware of diagnoses and treatment for mental health disorders. In some cases, judges don't take risk assessments seriously.

The prosecutors in my case were overzealous, to say the least. The prosecutors, along with the entire apparatus of the criminal justice system, worked against me in the early 2000s. The only difference between me and the countless other Black men in the criminal justice system was the differential balance in resources and relationships. I simply had more social capital than many other men in my predicament. I had powerful persons of influence standing behind me. My employer stood with me every step of the way. My counselor connected me with the sheriff, senior-level police administrators, and the district attorney in Dallas County.

System leaders need to listen more intently to all parties involved and take complaints seriously. In my case, there was a rush to judgment. I could not get Sophia the help that she desperately needed. Far too often, the criminal courts become involved in high-conflict custody cases. In my case, Lauryn attempted to use the criminal courts to help her win custody. It worked, at least temporarily.

During child custody hearings, judges should have a working knowledge of mental illness on both parties. It should not be the determining factor in awarding custody, but it should be a factor. Yet even when judges receive psychiatric reports, home study evaluations, psychological evaluations, and risk-assessment instruments, they should be taken seriously. Due to false allegations, I had supervised visits with Sophia once a week at a rate of $90 per hour. After I completed an Abel Assessment, I had unsupervised visits. Parents should not be forced to have supervised visits unless it is warranted. In my case, there was no basis for supervised visits.

Family court judges should exercise great care in determining the primary custody of the child. In my case, Judge Brenda Green was injurious in her decision-making. We did not receive an impartial hearing until the hearing with Judge Dorsey (Judge Dempsey in the book) in the Fulton County, Georgia, Superior Court.

Far too often, parents seeking custody of their child engage in "forum shopping." Lauryn wanted to have our case heard in the Dallas County family courts. The Dallas criminal and family courts had ruled in her favor from 2000–2004. She expected the same result when she ran from Georgia and attempted to have the jurisdiction of the case moved from Georgia to Texas. In the final analysis, her efforts were unsuccessful.

I cannot say enough about the harm that the prosecutors did under Dallas District Attorney Bill Hill's administration. Under his administration, convictions mattered more than the pursuit of justice. Both Craig Watkins and John Creuzot made much-needed reforms as Dallas County District Attorneys. Far too many prosecutors in America only care about convictions. Prosecutors should care about the administration of justice, not just convictions.

At last count, I spent over $250,000 on attorneys and related expenses. Without financial resources, I would have been just another Black man in America confined in our massive penal system.

The Child Protective Services system in both Dallas County, Texas and Fulton County, Georgia, did not respond to multiple requests to conduct investigations. I made several reports over a period of twelve years. On the other hand, Lauryn made one report, and the Texas Department of Family and Protective Services determined that there was "reason to believe" that neglectful supervision had occurred. This decision was overturned only after I appealed the decision (without an attorney).

The school systems also failed to intervene on Sophia's behalf. Sophia attended seven different schools in three cities. Lauryn would move Sophia to different schools as soon as I would start having visits with her at school. Several counselors, principals, assistant principals, and school administrators refused to act out of fear of retaliation from Lauryn. Schools are often the first line of defense for detecting physical abuse against children. Sophia often wore long-sleeved tops to hide the scars from her severe beatings. She often refused to wear gym shorts so that her cuts and lacerations would not be noticed. After the Amber Alert was issued, several parents and students called in to raise concerns about Lauryn's threats to her students.

Much has already been written about the collateral consequences of our massive criminal justice system. Michelle Alexander's book *The New Jim Crow* and Bryan Stevenson's book *Just Mercy* brought international attention to the problem of mass incarceration in the United States.

While I have been critical of many public system leaders, many of them got it right. I am thankful for Judge Dorsey in Atlanta (Fulton County). She refused to allow Lauryn to manipulate her. She appointed a guardian ad litem who really cared about children. She helped to save Sophia's life. She also provided me an opportunity to demonstrate that I could care for Sophia. Fathers have often received unfair treatment in the family courts. Much of this is due to many fathers choosing not to support their children. Yet there are countless fathers who want to be there for their children. We need to remove barriers so that men and women can have relationships with their children when warranted. Children need both parents in their lives. The Fulton County courts were willing to support whichever parent was most capable of caring for their children.

I am also thankful for the Cedar Hill Police Department. Detectives Valenti and Knott were there for us before and after the Amber Alert. They escorted my daughter to school for weeks and protected my family throughout the process. I also want to thank Jerry Varney. As a Dallas prosecutor, he was fair and did much to support my entire family.

Amid all this system failure, an angel by the name of Linett Franklin [Linda Forbes in the book] and her husband, Kevin, risked everything to help Sophia. They spoke up and spoke out and risked their lives in doing so. Linett was Lauryn's hairstylist and knew that Lauryn was not properly caring for Sophia. I refer to Linett as Sophia's "guardian angel."

After years of treatment, Sophia is doing well. She is a brilliant writer and is doing well in college. She is majoring in psychology. We have spent years getting her the best trauma therapy.

To the countless children who have experienced abuse, don't give up! Speak out! Speak up! Don't give in to the darkness! To God be the glory!

Resources

Baker, Amy, J. Michael Bone, and Brian Ludmer. 2014. *The High-Conflict Custody Battle*. Oakland: New Harbinger Publications.

Bockian, Neil, Valerie Porr, and Nora Elizabeth Villagran. 2002. *New Hope for People with Borderline Personality Disorder*. New York: Three Rivers Press.

Kreisman, Jerold, and Hal Straus. 2010. *I Hate You, Don't Leave Me: Understanding the Borderline Personality*. New York: Penguin Group.

Manning, Shari. 2011. *Loving Someone with BPD: How to Keep Out-of-Control Emotions from Destroying Your Relationship*. New York: The Guilford Press.

Mason, Paul T., and Randy Kreger. 2010. *Stop Walking on Eggshells: Taking Your Life Back When Someone You Care About Has Borderline Personality Disorder*. Oakland: New Harbinger Publications.

Roth, Kimberlee, and Freda Friedman. 2003. *Surviving a Borderline Parent: How to Heal Your Childhood Wounds and Build Trust, Boundaries, and Self-Esteem*. Oakland: New Harbinger Publications.

Williams, Terri M. 2008. *Black Pain: It Just Looks Like We're Not Hurting*. New York: Scribner.

Websites

American Psychological Association (Psychology Help Center), www.apa.org.
BPD Central, www.bpdcentral.com.
Childhelp National Child Abuse Hotline, www.childhelphotline.org
Diagnostic and Statistical Manual of Mental Disorders, Fifth Edition, www.psychiatry.org/psychiatrists/practice/dsm.
Gift from Within, www.giftfromwithin.org.
Hope for BPD, www.hopeforbpd.com.
National Alliance on Mental Illness (NAMI), www.nami.org.
National Association of Black Social Workers, www.nabsw.org.
National Resource Directory, www.nrd.gov.
National Sexual Violence Resource Center, www.nsvrc.org.
National Suicide Prevention Lifeline, www.suicidepreventionlifeline.org
Recovery Resources/National Education Alliance for Borderline Personality Disorder, www.borderlinepersonalitydisorder.org.
Substance Abuse and Mental Health Services Administration, www.samhsa.gov.
The Family Connections Program, www.borderlinepersonalitydisorder.com.
BorderlineDisorders.com, www.borderlinedisorders.com.